GAY PRIESTS

GAY PRIESTS

Edited by
JAMES G. WOLF

1817

Harper & Row, Publishers, San Francisco

New York, Grand Rapids, Philadelphia, St. Louis
London, Singapore, Sydney, Tokyo, Toronto

GAY PRIESTS. Copyright © 1989 by James G. Wolf. All rights reserved. Printed in the United States of America. No part of this book may be used or reproduced in any manner whatsoever without written permission except in the case of brief quotations embodied in critical articles and reviews. For information address Harper & Row, Publishers, Inc., 10 East 53rd Street, New York, NY 10022.

FIRST EDITION

^{_____}

Library of Congress Cataloging-in-Publication Data

Gay priests / edited by James G. Wolf.—1st ed.
    p. cm.
    Bibliography: p.
    Includes index.
    ISBN 0-06-069671-0
    1. Gay clergy. 2. Catholic Church—Clergy—Sexual behavior. 3. Homosexuality—Religious aspects—Catholic Church. I. Wolf, James G.
BX1912.9.G358   1989
253'.2—dc20   89-45235
                                                                      CIP

^{_____}

89 90 91 92 93 HAD 10 9 8 7 6 5 4 3 2 1

Contents

Tables

Foreword

JAY R. FEIERMAN, M.D.

To some people who see only the jacket of this book, the title, *Gay Priests*, will appear to be an irreconcilable paradox. People who have been taught and therefore believe that it is bad to be gay will have great difficulty reconciling the fact that many priests—whose lives are supposed to be exemplary and the personification of the life of Jesus Christ—have an "objective disorder," a much-publicized attribution recently bestowed upon all gay people through the official teaching of the Roman Catholic church.[1]

To some who actually read this book, the concept "gay priest" will cease to be a paradox; they will recognize that many of the thoughts and feelings that underlie same-sex attractions and affiliations really are the basic tenets of Christianity. This statement implies a distinction between being gay, that is, having the thoughts and feelings that predispose one toward same-sex attractions and affiliations, and being part of the urban gay subculture, a social subset of individuals that is more a reaction to prejudice and oppression than it is a reflection of being a gay person.

If certain members of the Roman Catholic clergy are outraged by the publication of this book or are embarrassed by its

Jay R. Feierman, M.D., is Clinical Associate Professor of Psychiatry at the University of New Mexico School of Medicine and Director of Research and Education in Behavioral Medicine for Presbyterian Healthcare Services, Albuquerque, New Mexico. For the past thirteen years, he has worked with Roman Catholic priests on personal mental-health and sexual issues and, in this capacity, has served as a consultant to numerous dioceses and religious orders throughout the United States.

content, those feelings must be considered self-inflicted wounds that must be dealt with compassionately. The outrage and embarrassment—which are transient, relatively superficial and easily directed at this book—overlie a deeper and more soul-wrenching feeling that lies within all gay priests irrespective of the degree to which they have "come out" to (been truthful with) other people about their homosexuality. That feeling is fear. It is the fear of discovery, of rejection, and saddest of all, of revealing themselves.

Theologians, who use the argument of authority and expect even educated nontheologians to believe what they say as an act of faith, have a moral responsibility to the people to whom they speak to be aware of the findings of modern science. It is painfully obvious to any biology-educated person of today who reads the theological literature on homosexuality that current theologians are not aware of these findings. Current Vatican usage of natural law, upon which so much of the theology of homosexuality is founded, is based neither on the field observations of naturalists nor on an understanding of even the fundamental principles and findings of modern behavioral biology (i.e., ethology). Rather, the Vatican's understanding of natural law is teleological in a narrow, physicalist sense. It ascribes goals to the Creator's design, including goals ascribed to behavior, that are based on the archaic concept of the ideal-type. This concept means that what is ideal for most individuals is necessarily ideal for all individuals. From the perspective of behavioral biology, the "goals of the Creator's design" implies that function follows anatomical form. This sequence, in large part, is backward in that through natural selection form originally follows function. Moreover, the ideal-type concept implies that a process such as natural or sexual selection should foster homogeneity and eliminate biological variability. Assuming that some of the variability in our sexual behavior is accounted for by genetic factors, if as a deliberate strategy we fostered homogeneity we could become an endangered species.

Because variety increases flexibility, our ability to adapt to change would be severely impaired.

It is in heterosexual behavior that the adaptive functions directly related to procreation reside ("adaptive" meaning "the capability of creating succeeding generations"). Therefore, homosexual behavior, if it were adopted as the exclusive form of sexual behavior in all individuals of a species, would not be adaptive. Yet our vertebrate ancestry has predisposed us to the building blocks of reptilian social structure: sex, dominance, and aggression. These remain intimately connected both in the behaviors they influence and in the structural relations within the primate brain, where the predispositions to nurturance and affiliation behaviors have evolved like the building blocks and also subserve social structure. Sexual motor patterns in nonhuman primates have been shown to have numerous nonprocreative functions such as the acknowledgment of social rank, the regulation of social tension, and the facilitation of social affiliation and reconciliation. Many nonhuman primates use sexual motor patterns as symbolic affiliative and rank-order gestures, not only between the sexes but also within sexes and even between generations.

It currently is not known whether homosexual behavior serves adaptive functions among adult humans. The question is legitimate, however, and eventually will be answered scientifically. What is known is that the predisposition toward the thoughts and feelings that predispose an individual toward homosexual behavior evolved in the context of natural selection and that the predisposition toward these thoughts and feelings is still present in the brain of about 10 percent of the human population. This prevalence is similar to the prevalence of some other behavioral traits of humans, such as left-handedness, and therefore is commensurate with homosexuality being a species-characteristic human trait.

Homosexual behavior in humans differs somewhat from homosexual behavior in most other social primates. In the majority of nonhuman social-primate species, all individuals engage in bisexual behavior; in humans, some individuals engage predominantly or exclusively in homosexual behavior. Recent neurohormonal research on numerous species, including humans, suggests that the degree to which an individual behaves in a masculine or a feminine manner (although modifiable through deliberation and practice) and the degree to which an individual is attracted to masculine or feminine attributes in other individuals is variable and is dependent largely upon varying amounts of hormones that perfuse the fetus in utero during the second and third trimesters of pregnancy when the brain is sexually differentiating.

Although there is an increase in sexual thoughts, feelings, and behavior (i.e., in the sex drive) associated with the hormonal surge of puberty, this surge merely raises the level of intensity of the drive. It does not influence the potential object of the drive. It seems that the object of the sex drive, that is, the attributes of individuals that one finds idiosyncratically erotic, is established before puberty by the organizational structure of the brain. This organizational structure, which can be seen both morphologically and physiologically, reflects the effects of two sets of factors. One set is the levels of internal fetal hormones that existed during the last two trimesters of pregnancy. These levels are those that influence the degree of masculine or feminine behavior of an individual and the degree of attraction of an individual to masculine or feminine attributes in other individuals. The other set is the type, frequency, and consequences of experiences that occurred during critical developmental periods in childhood in which learning can modify the hormonally induced predisposition.

In the attempt to resolve the seeming paradox of gay priests, it helps to realize that the word *religion* derives from the Latin root *religare*, which means "to bind together." It therefore is not paradoxical but, rather, quite understandable that men who feel attraction and affiliation toward their fellow men are the peacemakers and the men who feel called to the priesthood, where they can both live and preach this ideology. In today's world, human evolution is proceeding much faster by cultural transmission than by genetic transmission. If in the past two thousand years the message "turn the other cheek" represents evolutionary progress over "an eye for an eye and a tooth for a tooth," gay priests, who have been the standard-bearers and perhaps the originators of this message, have contributed to this progress.

Therefore, I ask you, the multitudes of gay priests for whom this book speaks, to have faith. The intentions of those of us who have contributed to this book are based on faith—in the wisdom and words of Jesus: "You shall know the truth and the truth shall set you free" (John 8:32).

I ask you, the persons reading this book who mainly want to know exactly what percentage of priests are gay, to carefully examine your own motivation. A question such as yours may tell as much about you as it asks about them.

Preface

JAMES G. WOLF

In 1976, John McNeill, a Jesuit priest, published *The Church and the Homosexual*, considered by many to be the first systematic critique of Roman Catholic doctrine on the topic from a theologian's perspective. Reaction from the Vatican was swift and effective: McNeill was forbidden from that point on to publicly voice his dissenting views on homosexuality. He obeyed the ruling until the fall of 1986, when Rome issued its stern warning, directed primarily at the bishops of the United States, that pastoral guidance was becoming too permissive regarding the acceptability of homosexuality. Feeling a moral obligation to speak up, McNeill decided to join others in their objections to this attempt by the Vatican to renew orthodox attitudes that stressed the impropriety of homosexuality. His decision to disobey Vatican orders left his superiors with no alternative. After nearly four decades as a Jesuit, the Rev. John McNeill was forced to leave the order.

As will be discussed throughout this collection of works, what happened to McNeill is but one highly publicized example of the steps that are taken against priests and religious who publicly express their dissent against contemporary Catholic moral theology. We therefore ask the reader to understand that the use of pseudonyms by the authors in part II is not a sly attempt to attract attention to our efforts by shrouding ourselves in mystery. The priests who wrote the essays in part II would most certainly jeopardize their current ministries, and quite possibly those of their superiors, if their names were made public. It is unfortunate that these men are not able to come forward to accept the acclaim and respond to the criticisms that no doubt will arise. Yet, it is this unfortunate state of affairs that, in our opinion, made our work necessary.

It is ironic that the Roman Catholic church has recently demonstrated so much public concern about the issue of homosexuality without any effort to acknowledge the considerable number of gay clergymen in the Church. Witness the strong public stand taken by American bishops against equal rights legislation in New York and Chicago, and witness the statement from the Vatican reasserting the opinion that a homosexual orientation is a sexual deviation and that homosexual activity is, without exception, immoral. Yet, we are unaware of any systematic effort by these same individuals to even acknowledge the fact that many of their own clergy, the spiritual counselors of the laity, are in fact gay.

Perhaps the bishops are unaware; most people probably are. More likely, members of the hierarchy are not unaware but find it too sensitive an issue to even begin admitting to themselves, much less to each other. Nevertheless, gay priests are an important, albeit unannounced, element within the Roman Catholic church and American society with their own outlook as well as their own needs and concerns that must be addressed. The purpose of this book is to bring issues to light.

The first point we had hoped to determine was whether or not there is indeed a significant number of gay priests in the United States. Occasionally an article or a book will suggest this, and it was certainly our opinion. But the question remained, Do the facts bear out these impressions? The "absolute" facts about homosexuality in any population will most likely remain elusive for some time. Thus, each of the authors has chosen to concentrate on particular issues that, taken together, cover a broad range of "probable" facts we are convinced will stand up to close scrutiny.

This book is proof that unorthodox issues often require unconventional strategies. The growing secular tolerance toward gay people in the United States contrasting with the increased rigidity of Catholic doctrine on homosexuality puts gay priests in a unique position. We felt that in order to provide the widest range of information and insight on the topic, we needed to take a dual approach, addressing the issue from a social science perspective, on the one hand, and from the gay priests' point of view, on the other.

Part I of this book is an analysis of responses by 101 gay priests to a questionnaire that I circulated throughout the United States while I was on staff at the University of Chicago's National Opinion Research Center. Intended to cover a variety of issues, the report in chapter 1 explores the consequences of Church doctrine and public opinion on these gay clergymen. It concludes with a discussion of the implications of the present situation for all gay clergy and for the Roman Catholic church as well. Though in no way intended to be the definitive statement on gay priests, my report attempts to outline some interpersonal, psychological, and spiritual concerns that appear to be productive topics for more extensive research.

The four chapters of part II, each written by a gay priest, are intended to set forth some of the personal and pastoral concerns felt to be most important. The gay clergy, like homosexual men and women in general, are at various levels of self-awareness. This has both positive and negative effects on their personal growth and development. In the first chapter of part II, "Invisible Gifts," the author concentrates on three main concerns. First, he outlines the various stages, and their associated problems, that many homosexual priests experience as they grow to accept themselves as gay men. Next he examines the implications of the timing of this awareness: whether it begins after ordination or before or during seminary training. The last section of the article stresses the complementary relation between characteristics of gay male sexuality and the religious life.

Next is a more autobiographical reflection entitled "A Christian Spirituality." Here the author examines the outcome of his many years of attempting to "act straight" and the impact it had on his relationships with others and on his own mental health. His discussion of how he resolved the conflict within himself, though informative to any interested reader, is intended to assist gay men and women facing the same spiritual dilemma.

The chapter "The Fears of a Gay Priest" is also autobiographical. The author describes his own personal and spiritual growth toward reconciliation of his religious beliefs and his sexual identity. As the title indicates, this author has chosen to concentrate on the fears he has faced and that are faced by many gay priests. He concludes with meditations on Scripture passages that are appropriate to the issues raised.

In the final chapter, "Where Do We Go from Here?" the author has chosen to focus on the current attitudes of the Church and society and the implications these have for open dialogue between gay clergy and their Church. Though recognizing "coming out" *en masse* as ill-advised, he offers advice to those "relatively few who choose to be more open" about their homosexuality. He in turn cautions those clergy who choose to remain deceptive about their sexual orientation of the restrictions this decision places on their own identity and, as a consequence, on their ability to be effective ministers.

Because there is so little available information on the topic of gay clergy, those who choose to write about it must rely on a variety of resources to break new ground. The purpose of having four gay priests (and a fifth who assisted in the editing of their work) reflect upon their personal lives was to articulate from their own experience points that they believed were generally applicable. This might appear to leave the reader with nothing more than idiosyncratic impressions and personal anecdotes. However, the particular men chosen have written from years of personal discussions and friendships with other gay priests, and each chapter has been reviewed and critiqued by several other gay priests and readers other than the authors.

By asking the authors of part II to work from their personal experience, we also hoped to describe the concerns of the gay priest more completely than is possible using the more "categorical" approach of the survey analysis. The first-person accounts are likely to help heterosexual persons better appreciate what it is like to be gay, especially a gay priest, in the United States. For the homosexual priest who thinks he is alone, the personal narratives should assure him that he is indeed not alone in his anxious search for a sense of personal and spiritual unity.

One of our assumptions is that homosexuality is, in and of itself, a healthy and acceptable orientation; that is, sexual attractions or acts between adults of the same sex in a loving relationship can be healthy and virtuous actions to be encouraged rather than condemned. This assumption is often debated, even though most mental health professionals no longer view homosexuality as a deviant orientation. However, we leave that debate for another forum. One does not have to accept that assumption in order to learn from our work. It should also be noted that the priests involved with this book, as well as many of the priests who responded to our survey, are not advocating a change in the traditional concept of celibacy. That debate, too, is for another forum. Here they speak as practicing celibates, presuming the Church discipline of celibacy for the clergy remains normative.

The reader will note the varying tone of the different chapters appearing this volume. Every attempt was made to be as objective as possible in conducting the research reported in part I. The research design, methodology, and analysis were presented and subjected to review at several University of Chicago seminars and at the national conference of the American Sociological Association in August 1987. By contrast, the chapters in part II were written with the express intention of assessing the impact of current Roman Catholic teaching and official actions from a gay priest's perspective. Review of the authors' work was extensive but conducted in a less public manner in order to protect their identity.

We look to the day when such anonymity is unnecessary. We hope for a time when churchmen and scholars alike are studying the issues in the spirit set forth by Pope Paul VI when he wrote, "One must not seek to conquer his questioner, but to convince him. In a sane and holy discussion there is no 'master' and no 'slave,' but two servants of the truth." The same truth, we assume, will set us all free.

The issue of the place of the homosexual in our society is today a much debated one. Since members of the gay community have become visible and assertive of their rights, the rest of society can no longer ignore them. Many books, from the scholarly to the renegade, have been published in the past few years exploring gay issues. This one focuses on a group that remains largely unnoticed and barely understood: the gay men of the Roman Catholic clergy.

Acknowledgments

The majority of the report appearing in part I was written while I was in graduate studies at the University of Chicago's Department of Sociology and a part-time staff member at the National Opinion Research Center, an environment that taught me early on that genuine intellectual controversy should be viewed as a barometer by which to measure the relative importance of any research agenda. Judging from the reaction I have received already from those with whom I have discussed this book, the topic, findings, and conclusions contained herein should prove to be of interest to academics, religious, as well as to other educated readers.

Though it is not possible for me to thank all those who helped me crystallize the ideas presented in part I, there are those who deserve particular mention. Wendy Griswold and Bill McCready not only provided the necessary guidance at the early stages of this research but also patiently reviewed several drafts leading up to the present chapter. William Julius Wilson also took time to review and comment on the final version. Without the benefit of their respective areas of expertise I most certainly would have been doomed to a quagmire of theoretical and methodological confusion.

The enthusiastic comments and criticisms to the initial presentation of my research design by Wendy, Dave Keer, and the other members of the Culture and Society Workshop (Spring 1984) forced me to reduce the naively panoramic scope of my plans to a more concrete and feasible project. Subsequent drafts of the questionnaire and study design were also aided by thoughtful comments from Lutz Erbring, Thomas Gannon, and Andrew Greeley. Gerald Suttles and the members of his Field Research Methods class helped me to arrive at a more succinct discussion format. I am grateful to Stuart Michael for his reaction to the work presented at the 1985 Spring Institute, as well as to Martin Weinberg and the other members of the Human Sexuality session who commented on my paper at the American Sociological Association national conference in Chicago in 1986. For providing me with access to and assistance with outside sources of data, I am indebted to my colleagues at the National Opinion Research Center, particularly Pat Bova and Tom Smith. The final version of the book took a more consistent and readable form through the efforts of Doug Mitchell and several anonymous reviewers Doug contacted for us. Finally, the many marginal notes and minute scrawled additions to early versions of the chapters in part II were deciphered and typed in a timely manner by Billie Crawford.

My wife, Karen, was always nearby with words of encouragement when things appeared to be falling apart. Her nightly view of the back of my head must have become tedious as I sat typing at our terminal or (quite often) merely staring at a blinking cursor with my chin in my hands. Her patience during this study is but one of the many things for which I am indebted to her.

It is unfortunately ironic that one of the main topics of this report is also that which prohibits me from naming those who are responsible for its completion: the priests who asked me to conduct the research and who provided the necessary financial support for it. It is truly rare for a graduate student to have such an important opportunity for research literally handed to him. Not only did I receive their full cooperation and funding, but I also was given *carte blanche* at every stage of the research. It was obvious from the first telephone call I received in February of 1984 that this group of priests did not merely want a report that would reflect what they wanted to hear; they were sincerely interested in finding out the truth as best we could determine it.

I will always be grateful for the opportunity these priests offered me at such an early stage in my career. Though I take full responsibility for any errors and omissions in my report, it has benefited greatly from the many meetings we have had over the years. I doubt that I will ever again have the chance to work with and for such a sincere and encouraging group of sponsors.

I. A SOCIOLOGICAL INVESTIGATION

1. Homosexuality and Religious Ideology: A Report on Gay Catholic Priests in the United States

JAMES G. WOLF

This chapter is an attempt to understand the experiences of gay Roman Catholic priests in the United States, both in terms of the situation as they face it as well as the implications that their beliefs, and their very existence, may have for their Church. I was first introduced to this project when a close friend of mine, a Catholic priest I had known for years, telephoned me in February of 1984 and told me of the book he and several others were starting to write about their experience as gay priests. He then asked if I would be willing to help them conduct a sample survey of priests to gather information on the elusive topic of sexuality and the priesthood. I had his added assurance that the members of his group were just as committed to handling this project with dignity as they were to getting their message out; the book was not intended to be a manifesto directed at Rome with "pens dipped in molten anger."

During the process of determining the issues to be included in the questionnaire and later in analyzing the responses we received, we were forced to evaluate a variety of cultural, social, and spiritual concerns that were all woven into the complex fabric of the central issue. I was obliged to consider the

3

legitimacy of religious authority, particularly in view of leading institutional scholars' disagreement about some of the most fundamental issues regarding sexuality. I knew our work would need to be conducted with caution because, like any Catholics who question the validity of Vatican teachings, we run the risk of being dismissed as radical troublemakers before our case is even heard. Moreover, for us to "fan the fire" of controversy over homosexuality without suggesting realistic and useful ways of dealing with the issue would be irresponsible. Most certainly, our goal was not to destroy the credibility of Church authority, yet we were well aware that the publication of work such as ours would probably force some sort of official response. We were intent on lifting the uneasy shroud of silence over this topic while at the same time maintaining a genuine spirit of concern for the future of our Church.

Finally, one of the most significant questions I had to resolve was that of the meaning of sexuality. I began the study with some rather naive ideas about homosexuality, as evidenced by my first draft of our questionnaire. As a gay friend of mine wisely pointed out to me, it would have provided a great deal of information about "who was doing what to whom and how often" but very little about what I now understand as sexuality. Simply put, my initial preoccupation was with trying to document sexuality as behavior. Ultimately, the psychological and spiritual components of a gay priest's life became the focal point of my research because of the central role they play in determining not only how these men view themselves but how they interact with others.

Rarely, if ever, are heterosexuals forced to try to determine whether or not their sexual orientation is valid. From puberty through old age, our awareness of an erotic attraction to members of the opposite sex is usually interpreted as a "natural" emotion, nothing to be concerned about in and of itself. The effect this emotion has on our relationships with others, as well as on our perception of ourselves, can only be calculated in terms of how often we have adjusted our activities to regulate our contact with certain others based (to whatever degree) on our level of attraction to them and how justified we feel in making these adjustments. All things being equal, it seems perfectly "natural" to most of us to desire association with someone we happen to find attractive.

Consider now the experience of homosexuals. From the moment they are first aware that they are erotically attracted to someone of their own sex until they accept their homosexuality as something good, they feel some level of anxiety that something is "wrong," that somewhere along the way, for whatever reason, they began proceeding in a different direction from most other people. Once gay people accept their homosexuality, they still may never feel comfortable telling anyone about this intensely personal aspect of their lives out of fear of being rejected because of it. They may carefully control their relationships in order to present a more socially acceptable image of themselves to others. The adjustments gay people make in their own social behavior, then, are affected not only by their level of erotic attraction to others but also by how comfortable they are with their sexual orientation and by how hostile to or tolerant of homosexuality they perceive the people around them to be.

The conclusion I could not avoid was that our sexuality, the aspect of ourselves determined by gender, sexual attraction, and sexual activity, can play a powerful role in determining our routine interactions with others depending on the extent to which we emphasize its importance. I suspect that for most heterosexuals sexuality is usually an unconscious component of personality that only becomes significant during times of fantasy or intimacy with another person. Though this is no doubt true for some gay men and women, the issue of sexuality is most likely much more conscious in their lives. Because of homosexuality's ongoing prominence in the mind of a gay person, sexuality, and all issues related to it, provides a near constant source of social and psychological ambiguities that one must address to maintain one's mental stability. For this reason

I feel safe in concluding that the average homosexual man or woman is far more qualified than the average heterosexual to assess the extent to which sexuality influences our psychological, social, and spiritual behavior.

In our culture a person usually does not accept a homosexual orientation until after a fair amount of soul-searching. If and when it is accepted, one must determine whether one's orientation is desirable. Moreover, whether or not it is interpreted as "good," the gay person is usually cautious (at least initially) about disclosing this "secret" to others and, if so, to whom. Consequently, sexuality plays a far more conscious role in the lives and minds of many gay people not because of anything physically or emotionally inherent in homosexuality *per se*, but because they realize that our cultural norms are at best only tolerant of, and at worst hostile to, homosexuality. It is for these reasons that we feel the issue of sexuality, and of homosexuality in particular, requires far more objective attention by the Roman Catholic hierarchy than it currently receives.

These are some of the more fundamental conclusions on which I based the report in this chapter. As the reader will find, the issue of sexual activity will be addressed, but it is by no means the central concern. Our primary focus is on the emotional component of sexuality as it affects the lives of gay priests. In addition to the psychological conflict faced by gay men and women just outlined, gay priests must face added pressure from the social expectations of anyone in the religious profession.

The behaviors associated with homosexuality are considered to be less than acceptable by the majority of Americans and are therefore not usually associated with ordained religious ministers.[1] What many fail to consider is the possibility that many of the men and women who have devoted themselves to the religious life are gay. It is therefore necessary to understand the personal concerns of gay priests and religious in order to appreciate the implications this situation has for the institutions they serve.

We have therefore attempted to explore the attitudes and behaviors of gay Roman Catholic priests in order to more fully understand their experiences as clergymen who knowingly (though usually not publicly) profess dual commitments, to the Catholic church and to their own sexual identity. The original survey data analyzed below was collected over a one-year period via a mailed questionnaire that had been circulated among friends who were all gay priests. It suggests several tentative conclusions.

Homosexuality and dedication to the priesthood are not mutually exclusive. The majority of the priests who responded to our questionnaire appear to be as devoted to the Church as they are to their belief in the legitimacy of their own sexual identity. In their private lives, clandestine behavior is quite common. The majority, however, report they probably would not become actively involved in an organized attempt to open a dialogue with Church authorities on the issue of sexuality and the priesthood.

The gay priests we heard from report the same level of happiness and likelihood of remaining in the priesthood as priests in general. That is to say, their lives are not best described as chronic and silent suffering. On the contrary, their spiritual, personal, and professional lives present a dynamic scenario of men who have found a great deal of fulfillment mixed with varying levels of frustration. Although much of this frustration results from the traditionally defined and often constraining attitude toward sexuality found in the Church, the pressures associated with having taken the vow of celibacy are also a major concern for these priests.

For the most part, the respondents have accepted the fact that they are gay and are thankful for it, often referring to their homosexuality as a "gift" that most others will never enjoy. These priests have communicated that they are gay to at least some other people (which is the only way they could have fallen into the sample), and they are willing to take a certain amount of risk for what they believe in by participating, albeit anonymously, in our study.

In order to best appreciate the contribution as well as the limitations of the original data presented here from the network sample of gay priests, the reader must keep in mind that this study is mainly exploratory and intended to provide a first look at an issue that deserves far more extensive research than we were able to carry out. The results of our survey are not representative for all gay priests, because the sample was not random. That is, this was a self-selected group of gay priests, each of whom knew at least one of the other respondents. A more complete description of the methodology and of technical issues related to the collection and analysis of the data used in this study is presented in the Appendix.

Unfortunately, we have no way of determining how many gay priests were contacted by friends but refused to participate, for whatever reason. Nonresponse was most likely due to several reasons that are common in survey research: disagreement with the expressed necessity or perceived goals of the study, uncertainty about their ability to maintain anonymity, and/or lack of faith that the results would be presented in a correct manner. Other more personal reasons could have certainly played a role in nonparticipation as well, such as problems with self-acceptance or disclosure to others, even in an anonymous questionnaire. The fact remains that we have unique information about 101 gay priests with which to begin understanding what they face as clergymen.

The body of scientific literature on homosexuality has grown dramatically over the past twenty-five years, yet almost none of it deals specifically with the gay clergy. Although much has been written on the topic of homosexuality and the teachings of the Church, most of this literature is theological in nature and of little use when attempting to determine how the issue is actually being resolved by those who are gay and who also have committed themselves to the religious life of a priest. It is toward this question I have devoted this study.

Chapter 1 is divided into four sections. The first provides a historical context, emphasizing that contemporary ethics regarding homosexuality have grown out of many centuries of traditional beliefs, whereas the current controversy over the legitimacy of Roman Catholic doctrine on this matter has been the topic of public debate only in the very recent past. Following is a comparison of the responses by members of our sample with those of a random sample of over five thousand priests. The next section takes a closer look at attitudinal and behavioral issues of specific importance to our study. The last section concludes the chapter by outlining some of the more important implications of the study's findings for gay priests and for the Church.

Historical Issues

Although the primary purpose of this chapter is to focus attention on the effects of "Catholic culture" on gay Catholic priests, we are in no way implying that the founding of Christianity was the genesis of what is considered the "Catholic attitude" regarding homosexuality. The published proceedings of a seminar on Western sexuality contain works that repeatedly point out that early Judeo-Christian theologians were not introducing new ideas about sexuality.[2] Essays by Michel Foucault, Paul Veyne, Philippe Ariès, and Michael Pollack appearing in that volume discuss the various aspects of religious and social tolerance of sexual behavior that have been developing over thousands of years.

What emerges from their combined efforts is a description of a system of sexual attitudes that is rooted in the earliest recorded thought of the Stoics and Neoplatonics, diffused throughout western Europe and refined by the world's religions. Of course, other social forces have played a role in shaping public sentiment toward proper sexual conduct, but because the presence of homosexuality presents no clear threat to political or economic stability, this battle against what seems abnormal or "somehow just not right" has taken place primarily in the arena of religion.

As is true of the other world religions of our time, the foundation of any moral teaching of the Roman Catholic church is to be found in its sacred scriptures. The Holy Bible is the source of passages that most conservative theologians and members of the Church hierarchy cite as proof that homosexuality is against God's will. The Rev. Richard Wagner, whose research will be reviewed extensively below, cites some of the more commonly quoted Scripture passages as well as passages from classic theologians.[3]

The section of Genesis recounting the downfall of Sodom and Gomorrah (19:4–11) tells of how Lot had to forcibly defend men visiting his home from the sexual advances of the townsmen. This passage has led many to assume that homosexuality was one of the main reasons for the destruction of these cities. Other Old Testament passages (Leviticus 18:22; 20:13) decry homosexual activity as an "abomination" punishable by death. The letters attributed to Paul in the New Testament also contain teachings on homosexual acts that state that those who behave in such a manner "will not fall heir to the Kingdom of God" (1 Corinthians 6:9), that they are ignoring the word of God (1 Timothy 1:10), and that in giving in to such "disgraceful passions" they will receive the "penalty for their perversity" (Romans 1:26–27). Immoral behavior is the main concern of these passages; the emotional dimensions of homosexuality and their possible legitimacy are ignored. However, highly regarded biblical scholars conclude that many of the references to homosexuality found in contemporary versions of the Bible are actually based on very ambigious terms used in the original Greek and Hebrew writings.[4]

The general consensus of the noted Catholic theologians of the first three centuries after the death of Christ (known as the patristic period) was that homosexual activity is a direct violation of God's will. Men such as John Chrysostom and Augustine referred to it as "the most severe of all plagues," which "ought everywhere and always to be detested and punished."[5]

By the thirteenth century, denouncement of homosexuality had become institutionalized in canon law due in no small part to the work of Thomas Aquinas. One of his major "scientific" arguments in support of the conclusions reached by the patristic theologians was that because homosexual acts are not to be found among the lower animals, such activity cannot be considered natural among human beings.

Continuing up to the mid-twentieth century, Christian theologians in general were still referring to homosexuality as a spiritual and emotional handicap. It is important to note that clearer distinctions were being made between the gravity of a homosexual orientation and the sin associated with homosexual activity, sometimes referred to as "homosexualism."[6] However, the traditional teaching of homosexuality as unequivocally immoral went essentially unchallenged until the latter half of the twentieth century.

The emergence of the gay rights movement in Western society, combined with the reform-minded atmosphere surrounding the Second Vatican Council, opened the way for opposition to traditional Church teaching. At this time literature emerged that ranged from "a cautious reassessment" to "the first systematic attack" on the theological foundations of the Catholic church's position on homosexuality.[7] It was at around this time that powerful secular organizations, mainly the American Psychiatric Association and the American Psychological Association, announced that homosexuality was no longer to be considered an abnormality but a legitimate sexual orientation. Since that time the issue of homosexuality and of the role of gay people within the Church has remained an unresolved controversy.

A conservatively oriented review of the few official statements by Church authorities on homosexuality reveals that the official stance of the Church regarding homosexual activity has changed little since the patristic period.[8] The review notes that Pope John Paul II praised the bishops of the United States for correctly making the distinction, in their pastoral letter "To Live in Christ" (approved by the assembly of bishops in 1976), between homosexual activity and a homosexual orientation; the former being immoral, the latter being a temptation to sin. This was apparently the first time the head of the Catholic church made it clear that to be gay was not a sin but merely a propensity toward sinfulness that presents a constant struggle. It is clear that the Church views homosexuality as an affliction rather than a legitimate sexual orientation.[9]

The review's in-depth study of gays and the Catholic church is intended to function as an alarm to concerned Catholics everywhere about the current well-organized "infiltration" of gays into all levels of the American church.[10] It also provides a detailed account of the growth and the breadth of confusion over this issue faced by the gay priest. The author presents lists of Catholic bishops and organizations who have been cited by gay sympathizers as supportive of gay rights in the Church, names of priests and religious who have been publicly pro–gay rights and consequently "silenced" or removed from their duties by their superiors, quotes from respected Church scholars supporting changes in doctrine followed by counter-arguments by equally respected scholars, personal letters and interoffice memoranda of various Catholic organization officials promoting one or the other side of the debate, and an apparently exhaustive list of the local chapters of Dignity (the pro-gay Catholic organization) as well as other Catholic organizations that are actively voicing their support for greater acceptance of gay people by the Church.

Homophobia in the Church has jeopardized the careers of many priests who still remain active in the pro–gay rights movement directed specifically at Catholic moral theology. Two major administrative reports, one published by an archdiocese and the other by a state-level Catholic conference, concluded by challenging the current "official" stand of the Church on the acceptability of homosexuality, the same challenges that individual religious activists have been punished for promoting.[11]

The situation faced by the gay priest, therefore, is one of growing confusion and apparent contradiction. The pope has reconfirmed the traditional teaching of almost two millennia, yet the opinions of our society in general, along with those of a growing number of Catholics, have moved toward a more tolerant view of homosexuality during the last fifteen years. In this social environment the gay priest is likely to feel justified in accepting himself as gay, yet unlikely to admit this acceptance publicly for fear of recriminations by members of the very organization he has chosen to serve.

Although debates and conclusions of Church theologians and officials are certainly of great importance to the gay priest, the determination by Church leaders of what is and is not appropriate is also significantly affected by the opinions of the Catholic congregation. One of the many goals of Catholic church officials is to provide followers with guidelines for good living in an ever-changing world. It is a fallacy, however, to believe that these guidelines are arrived at without any recognition of the current beliefs and activities of those followers. Specifically, the homosexuality debate in the Catholic church during the 1970s emerged not long after the spread of the gay liberation movement, which began to flourish in the late 1960s. The challenge most probably did not arise until then because gay rights was a "nonissue" with Church leaders. Prior to that time the challenges were small, isolated, and without cultural sympathy and therefore were easily dismissed.

To understand the pattern of beliefs about homosexuality faced by gay priests in the parishes, schools, hospitals, and other institutions in which they work and live, we may consult the General Social Survey (GSS), a national survey of randomly selected U.S. citizens since 1972. The graph shows only the responses of the Catholics in the samples taken each year, though the trends are quite similar in the U.S. population as a

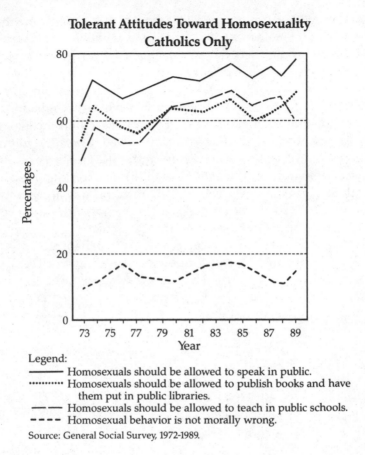

Tolerant Attitudes Toward Homosexuality
Catholics Only

Legend:
——— Homosexuals should be allowed to speak in public.
·········· Homosexuals should be allowed to publish books and have
      them put in public libraries.
—— — Homosexuals should be allowed to teach in public schools.
- - - - Homosexual behavior is not morally wrong.
Source: General Social Survey, 1972-1989.

whole. What is perhaps most striking about these results is the
very clear separation between support for protecting the civil
liberties of gay people and the belief that homosexual activity is
not morally wrong.

Each of the changes shown in the four trends were found to
be statistically significant over the past sixteen years: about .06
percent per year for attitudes about homosexual behavior and
between .5 and .8 percent per year for the questions about civil
liberty issues. Although an increasing number of Catholics are
supporting the protection of the civil liberties of gay people, the

proportion who feel homosexual activity is not morally wrong remains much smaller and more stable. That is, an increasing number of Catholics are expressing support for gay rights but not for gay sexual activity.

This is but one example of the "public versus private" morality. In their analysis of historic and recent issues related to individualism and commitment, the sociologist Robert Bellah and his colleagues discuss religion as one of the many social institutions that have been transformed by the strong (though sometimes disruptive) American ethic of personal freedom.[12] No longer is religion the all-encompassing guide to cultural and political decisions that it was for the Congregationalist founders of our nation. In essence, religion now has its effects on the personal feelings of individuals regarding an issue, opinions that people may feel very strongly about but do not feel should be translated into legal mandates. Catholics may therefore privately believe that homosexuality is unacceptable, but only a small minority would wish to see legal (i.e., secular) sanctions taken against gay people for their behavior.

Throughout the centuries public sentiment regarding homosexuality has ranged from casual ambivalence to outright persecution. Until very recently gay men and women organized their activities to protect their self-interest only on the rarest occasions, and then only in small, fragmented groups. The emergence of the gay rights movement as a legitimate political force marked the beginning of a radically new agenda for public debate.[13] Legislators were forced to reassess the constitutionality of previously unchallenged sanctions against gay people just as religious leaders soon found themselves confronted with the need to either justify or redefine their official teachings regarding the morality of homosexuality. The post–Vatican II era of reform in the Roman Catholic church during the late 1960s and early 1970s was also the beginning of Catholic theological debate over homosexuality that continues to the present. As with many public debates, the controversy has caused a variety of strong emotional responses, both positive and negative.

The spiritual and social environment for gay priests in this country is clearly a shifting mixture of tolerance and condemnation, sympathy and rejection, an environment that uniquely affects their attitudes and behavior. The remainder of this chapter will examine how these priests have managed (or tried to manage) their lives as members of the American Catholic clergy. The next section explores the spiritual, personal, and interpersonal experiences of gay priests and those of priests in general through a comparison of the gay priests who participated in our survey with a sample of priests who were surveyed in a study sponsored by the National Conference of Catholic Bishops.

Gay Priests and All Priests Compared

As with other studies of gay males, this study found the collection of adequate data to be a challenging task, a task made even more formidable by our target population's being the Catholic clergy.[14] Ideally we should have received responses from a random sample of all priests in the United States; these would have made possible many important comparisons between gay and nongay priests. Not surprisingly, our attempt at such a random sample, discussed in the Appendix, proved unsuccessful.

The alternative used in this study was a network sample consisting only of gay priests. Each of the priests involved in initiating this research contacted numerous friends who were also gay priests and sent them copies of the questionnaire with instructions to make and forward copies of it to other gay priests, who were in turn asked to carry on the process. Notices were also placed in two newsletters, one for gay Catholics and the other for gay Catholic clergy, asking any gay priest wishing to participate in our study to submit his name and address so that we could mail him a questionnaire. These two methods produced 104 responses, but three were excluded from the analysis: two were from heterosexual priests; the other was sent by a man who had left the priesthood.

The problem with a "snowball" sample such as ours is the researcher's inability to determine the extent to which the data are biased. Respondents are chosen by other respondents and, without intervention by the researcher, are free to choose whether or not they will cooperate. The analyst is then left to speculate about how many chose not to participate and why. One cannot justifiably assume that nonresponse was random nor that responses adequately reflect the experiences of the whole population in question. Keeping the following characteristics of our respondents in mind, however, we feel that the results presented in this chapter can be used to inform more productive discussion and research because of the types of gay priests who did participate in our survey.

First, our respondents have disclosed their homosexual identity to others and have therefore identified themselves as members of a minority group; in some cases they have identified with the active gay subculture. If there is evidence of a "sociosexual militancy" to be found among gay priests it would most likely be among men like these who have decided to admit their gay sexuality to themselves rather then among those gay priests who have yet to define themselves as homosexuals. Second, our sample is also from among those gay men who have decided to remain in the priesthood. From them we can get an impression of how this decision affects professional commitment and private resolution. Of concern here is the manner in which they have resolved the obvious conflict between their personal acceptance of their own sexual orientation and the institutional traditions to which they are assumed to have committed themselves. Finally, many of the extraneous variables of concern in other studies are held nearly constant by the nature of our sample. Factors such as sex, marital status, occupation, and religious affiliation are stable. There are probably only minor variations in educational attainment; each of the respondents is assumed to have attained at least a college degree.

In addition to our sample, we will use for comparative purposes the results of a survey commissioned by the Ad Hoc Committee on Pastoral Research and Practices of the National Conference of Catholic Bishops (NCCB). This was a national survey, conducted by the National Opinion Research Center (NORC) in 1970, that produced from a random sample of Roman Catholic priests well over five thousand responses to questions regarding attitudes, behavior, and experiences associated with priestly life. Since the proper scientific methods were used to select the NCCB sample, it is considered representative of all priests at that time. Although somewhat dated, it does provide a useful "yardstick" with which to measure the results of our original data. In deciding which questions from the NCCB survey to include in our questionnaire, care was taken to include only those questions that dealt with general attitudes and opinions. Hereafter, the results of the 1970 survey will be referred to as from the NCCB sample.[15]

In order to facilitate the comparison of our data with the NCCB sample, a simple rule will be used throughout: differences of around 15 percent will be considered noteworthy; those in excess of 25 percent will be discussed as important. This is not to imply that they are to be thought of as statistically significant but only as relatively large differences. Our questionnaire is reproduced in the Appendix, which also includes a discussion of why the commonly used tests of statistical significance are inappropriate for our data.

Demographics

Before examining the results of our study, it is important to understand who our respondents are compared with priests in general. Comparison of the information on the priests in both samples (see Table 1) indicates a wide distribution for our sample in geographic location and type of position to which they are currently assigned; the distributions for the most part are similar to those of the NCCB data. Note the slightly higher than expected response rates from the Midwest; these are inflated by the fact that the Midwest was the point of origin for circulating the questionnaire.

Table 1 shows that our sample is younger, slightly more likely to be in a large city and/or a member of a religious order than would have been expected if our sample had been a random sample of all priests. These results most likely reflect the fact that the priests responsible for initiating the distribution of the questionnaire were mostly younger members of religious orders currently living in major urban areas. These factors were controlled for during the exploratory stage of data analysis but were not found to be of any notable importance. That is, the differences in age, residency, or affiliation with diocese or order were not found to be important explantory factors, for our data or the NCCB sample, in the comparisons that will be described in this chapter.

Of the official activities to which priests are currently assigned, the results suggest that our sample may underrepresent the "traditional" parish priest, though the number holding other types of positions appears to be proportionally similar. An optional question asked the respondent to list the highest position(s) ever held while a priest. Over thirty unique combinations of positions were listed: parish pastor (by far the most common), a variety of administrative positions within religious orders as well as in dioceses, priors of orders, directors of seminaries and novitiates, high school principals, university professors, and, in one case, simply "a *high* position." There is, therefore, no evidence to suggest that gay priests are to be found in any particular age group, location, affiliation, or type of assignment.

Spirituality

Just as creativity is often the driving force behind a successful artist, spirituality can be considered the lifeblood of a priest. A

Table 1.

Percentages for Demographic Information on Respondents
to Network and NCCB Surveys

	Network (N = 101)	NCCB (N = 5475)
AGE		
35 or less	28.7%	25.3%
36–45	40.6	29.0
46–55	19.8	23.4
56 or over	10.9	22.3
REGION[a]		
New England	6.9%	10.4%
Mid Atlantic	14.9	19.6
E. North Central	21.8	19.3
W. North Central	17.8	12.5
South Atlantic	10.9	7.5
E. South Central	0.0	1.7
W. South Central	3.0	8.1
Mountain	7.9	4.2
Pacific	16.8	9.3
Outside U.S.	0.0	7.4
LOCATION		
Urban	57.4%	34.1%
Suburban	21.8	22.5
Rural	20.8	43.4
AFFILIATION		
Diocesan	47.5%	55.6%
Religious Order	52.5	38.5
Bishop or Major Superior[b]	N.A.	5.8
CURRENT ASSIGNMENT[c]		
Parish Work	48.5%	65.7%
Counselor	26.7	23.4
Teacher	25.7	30.5
Administrator	22.8	20.9
Student	13.9	11.8
Chaplain	8.9	15.8
Monk	5.0	5.7
Other	14.9	19.1

NOTE: Percentages do not add to 100 due to rounding.

[a]Region (U.S. Census classifications) determined from postmark on questionnaire.

[b]Category not available in network survey.

[c]Multiple responses allowed.

sterile or conflicting spiritual life could rapidly lead to a confused or cynical existence. This could be particularly problematic for a man who is expected to be an exemplary Catholic by almost anyone who knows he is a priest. In the context presented here, spirituality refers to positive and inspirational experiences as well as to those deemed negative or undesirable.

Respondents were asked to report how often they had experienced each of six types of spiritual phenomenon during the previous two or three years. Table 2 compares the results of the two surveys, listing the proportions of those who reported any of these experiences in ascending order of differences between the two samples. Although the rank ordering of the frequencies within each sample are identical, from almost all having felt to be in the presence of God down to less than half ever feeling afraid of God, the absolute differences between the two groups for each type varied from almost no difference (ever felt in the presence of God) to a difference of over 20 percent (ever felt abandoned by God).

Of the positive experiences of feeling in the presence of, loved by, or at one with God, there were higher proportions of gay priests reporting in the affirmative than in the NCCB sample. Note that the overwhelming majority of priests in both samples reported having experienced these positive spiritual phenomena, thus the difference between the two samples is not considered to be of great significance.

A comparison of the responses regarding negative spiritual experiences does show notable differences between the two samples. The proportion of gay priests reporting ever having felt being abandoned by God (42.6%) was twice as high as for the NCCB sample (21.1%). And yet, whereas only half of the gay priests responded ever feeling tempted by the devil, two-thirds of the NCCB sample reported feeling so.

These feelings suggest that the gay priests in our sample enjoy the same high level of positive spiritual experiences as priests in general. The differences are to be found in the negative aspects of spirituality. Priests in the NCCB sample appear to be more troubled than gay priests by feelings of being seduced toward evil by the devil (or, it is presumed, by other sources of temptation). The priests in our sample, by contrast, seem more prone to feelings of spiritual isolation than priests in the NCCB sample. The distinction between being tempted away from God and being rejected by God is a significant one. The problem of rejection (or fear of rejection) emerged throughout the study as a major concern for gay priests.

Table 2.

Percentages of Respondents Experiencing Various Spiritual Phenomena

RESPONDENTS WHO, IN THE LAST TWO OR THREE YEARS,
HAVE AT LEAST ONCE FELT

	Network	NCCB	Difference
a) in the presence of God	99.0% (100)	96.6% (5300)	2.4%
b) afraid of God	44.6 (101)	40.1 (5127)	4.5
c) loved by God	98.0 (101)	91.2 (5234)	6.8
d) at one with God	95.0 (101)	81.5 (5179)	13.5
e) abandoned by God	42.6 (101)	21.1 (5170)	21.5
f) tempted by the devil	48.5 (101)	67.2 (5166)	18.7

NOTE: Percentages are based on the number of respondents in each survey, which appear in parentheses.

Satisfaction

The life of a priest is multidimensional, encompassing not only the personal aspects of spirituality and responsibilities of the priesthood but nonreligious and interpersonal aspects as well. This section deals with responses to questions about various sources of satisfaction for priests. In order to more easily understand these responses, as well as those in the next section, sources of frustration, the issues will be discussed in terms of two dichotomies: intrapersonal/interpersonal and vocational/nonvocational. Intrapersonal refers to the psychological dimension, whereas the interpersonal refers to activities with other people. Issues related to priestly responsibilities were also found to be quite different in nature from those outside these responsibilities. These classifications are in no way intended to be considered mutually exclusive, but only as a useful way to summarize responses to what may appear to be a large set of unrelated issues.

The various sources of satisfaction presented in the surveys are shown in Table 3. The percentages are of those describing each of these issues as "frequent" sources of satisfaction for them, listed in ascending order of the differences between the two surveys. The first three of the seven subjects represented, in which differences are less than 15 percent, are all considered to fall into the category of a priest's professional responsibilities. Administering the sacraments and the respect received from others show almost no difference between the two groups, whereas administrative work and the fifth topic, spiritual security of being a priest, appears more important for priests in the NCCB sample than for our sample of gay priests.

Most of the topics where the difference is most notable in Table 3 are not necessarily related to a priest's professional responsibilities. The development of friendships and engaging in efforts of social reform both involve interpersonal activities, but large differences are found in the areas of spiritual security and intellectual and creative activities as well. Less than one-fourth of our respondents cited the spiritual security of the priesthood as a frequent source of satisfaction, half as large as the proportion found in the NCCB sample. About one-half of the NCCB sample stated creative activities were a frequent source of satisfaction, compared with nine-tenths of our sample.

There was no agreement in the rank of most to least

important of these seven topics within each of the two samples. However, in both samples, over half the respondents reported that administering the sacraments, developing close friendships, and intellectual activities were frequently satisfying experiences. Also, in our sample, over half reported that engaging in efforts of social reform was frequently fulfilling.

Table 3.

Percentages of Respondents Reporting Selected Topics as Frequent Sources of Satisfaction, Network and NCCB Samples

	Network	NCCB	Difference
a) Administering the sacraments	77.3% (101)	80.6% (5419)	3.3%
b) Respect received for being a priest	29.7 (101)	23.2 (5398)	6.5
c) Administrative work	18.8 (101)	32.0 (5209)	13.2
d) Developing friendships	90.0 (100)	71.8 (5324)	18.2
e) Spiritual security of being a priest	23.4 (98)	46.3 (5324)	22.9
f) Engaging in efforts of social reform	55.4 (101)	22.1 (5198)	33.3
g) Intellectual and creative activities	90.1 (94)	50.8 (5326)	39.3
h) Leading a celibate life*	8.5 (94)	N.A.	—
i) Hobbies*	68.0 (100)	N.A.	—

NOTE: Percentages based on number in parentheses.
*Question not asked in NCCB survey.

In sum, the sources of fulfillment are not notably different for the two samples when comparing factors related to responsibilities of the priesthood. Notable differences did emerge, however, with topics less oriented to clerical concerns. In particular, our sample, in significantly higher proportions than the NCCB sample, cited intellectual, political, and social sources of satisfaction. Although their level of enjoyment in administering the sacraments is essentially as high as for those in the NCCB sample, the gay priests we heard from appear to gain even more happiness from their personal and social lives.

Two additional topics were presented in our questionnaire. Whereas two-thirds of the priests in our sample reported that they frequently enjoyed their personal hobbies, less than 9 percent stated that celibacy was a frequent source of satisfaction. This latter result is not surprising in light of further examination of the celibacy issue discussed later in the chapter.

Problems

For each of the six topics presented in both surveys as possible sources of problems for the respondents, the proportions reporting them as frequently problematic were two to three times higher for our sample than the NCCB sample, with the exception of celibacy, where the proportions were over five times higher. As the list in Table 4 shows, the rank ordering within each sample from least to most frequently a source of problems is identical for each topic except celibacy. Celibacy was the biggest problem of the six for our respondents but ranked only fourth in the NCCB sample. The smallest differences between the two samples were generally on topics related to professional responsibilities involving relationships with other people. The two largest differences were on topics of a more personal nature: loneliness and celibacy. Though we have not considered loneliness here to be professionally related, this categorization is tenuous; loneliness has many possible causes.

In view of the fact that the rank ordering of the topics (excluding celibacy) is the same for both samples, the differences shown in Table 4 support the conclusion that the gay priests in our sample feel much more affected by frustration than priests in the NCCB sample. One should not conclude that these frustrations outweigh the fulfillment gay priests enjoy in their lives, but only that they may be more sensitive to possible sources of problems than priests in general.

Table 4.

Percentages of Respondents Reporting Selected Topics as Frequent Sources of Problems, Network and NCCB Samples

	Network	NCCB	Difference
a) Lack of personal fulfillment	21.0% (100)	8.4% (5342)	12.6%
b) Relevance of the work priests do	26.0 (100)	9.0 (5237)	17.0
c) Relations with superiors	32.0 (100)	11.5 (5337)	20.5
d) Authority structure of the Church	52.0 (100)	24.7 (5400)	27.3
e) Loneliness of priesthood	44.0 (100)	14.8 (5422)	29.2
f) Leading a celibate life	63.0 (100)	11.0 (5422)	52.0
g) Psychosexual development*	34.0 (99)	N.A.	—
h) Relevance of certain Church doctrine*	56.0 (100)	N.A.	—
i) Inability to develop friendships*	19.0 (100)	N.A.	—

NOTE: Percentages based on number in parentheses.
*Question not asked in NCCB survey.

Three topics were included in our questionnaire that did not appear in the NCCB study. Only about two in ten of our respondents reported that they frequently had problems developing close personal friendships, with roughly the same proportion listing this as an occasional problem. One-third stated that their psychosexual development was problematic, and two-thirds were frustrated by the relevancy of certain Church doctrine. Though this last topic could refer to many things, verbatim responses indicate that the Church's teaching on homosexuality is probably what most were referring to in this response.

The findings related to psychosexual development are of particular concern. A team of psychologists studying Roman Catholic priests, part of the same project that sponsored the NCCB survey, found this aspect of a priest's psychological profile to be the most important of twenty-eight personality characteristics used in determining whether or not a priest had a well-developed personality.[16] Because one-third of our sample expressed frequent difficulty with their psychosexual development, with an additional 29.3 percent reporting occasional problems in this area, our findings suggest that gay priests may find it difficult to maintain a healthy attitude about themselves and their relationships with others.

Psychological problems experienced by gay priests should not be understood as necessarily caused by the apparent dissonance between homosexuality and religious convictions. An international survey of gay men found evidence that devoutly religious gay men often successfully managed to resolve the potential ideological conflict between gay and religious viewpoints:

> It was expected that the conflict between religiosity and sexuality would result in greater psychological problems for religious homosexuals. Other than showing greater guilt, shame, or anxiety after their first homosexual experience, however, this was not the case. We found that many religious homosexuals *reinterpret religion as not violated by homosexuality.*[17]

As one might assume, theological reinterpretation and the ability to "compartmentalize" their sexual lives from the rest of their responsibilities are common phenomena among the priests in our sample.

Other Comparisons

The last two comparisons deal with general attitudes regarding the respondents' personal happiness and plans for the future. The results of these two questions are not only of interest by themselves but also provide a useful summary of the comparisons of these two groups of priests so far.

The results presented in the first half of Table 5 are the proportions of priests answering the question "Are you generally happy or unhappy with your life?" On average, the gay priests in our sample appear to be happier than priests in 1970. The most important difference between the two samples is among those who actually state that are unhappy: 4.0 percent in our sample versus 15.4 percent in the NCCB sample.

Table 5.

Percentages of Responses Regarding Happiness and Future Plans in the Priesthood, Network and NCCB Samples

	Network (N = 100)	NCCB (N = 5419)	Difference
GENERAL LEVEL OF HAPPINESS			
Very Happy	25.7%	28.4%	2.7%
Happy	70.3	56.2	14.1
Not Very Happy	4.0	15.4	11.4
FUTHER PLANS IN THE PRIESTHOOD			
Probably/Definitely Stay	82.2%	88.8%	6.6%
Uncertain	12.9	8.3	4.6
Probably/Definitely Leave	5.0	2.9	2.9

The responses in the second half of Table 5 are to a more specific question about whether or not the respondent intends to remain in the priesthood. Although the responses of the gay priests are slightly higher for the "uncertain" or "leave" categories, there does not appear to be any dramatic deviation from the responses of priests in the NCCB survey. Age appears to explain the small differences here. Younger priests in both samples are more prone to be considering leaving, and the average age of our sample was less than that of the NCCB sample. The results presented in this table thus reveal that in spite of the more notable differences discussed so far, gay priests seem to be quite happy with their lives and are about as likely to plan on remaining in the priesthood as are priests in general.

The written comments of some of our respondents suggest that those who indicate their future was uncertain do intend on remaining in the priesthood as long as the situation does not become intolerable.[18]

I love the priesthood and work by the Church; to leave would be the hardest thing in my life. I have been in love and when in love have been sexually active with my lover. Church structure brings a lot of tension to a love relationship. I don't think I can survive as a human without a lover. If Church authorities force the issue with me, I'll leave the priesthood to keep my freedom to be in a loving relationship.

When I said [in response to a question in the survey] that I am "uncertain" about my future [in the priesthood], I mean that (a) I could reach a point where the loneliness may be too great, or (b) institutional pressure may increase. Conservatism and rigidity seem to be on the rise.

Given the current antihomosexual bias of Catholic ideology, one might ask why a gay male would choose to remain in the priesthood. One of the founders of New Ways Ministry (a major organization for gay/lesbian religious) was ordered by the Vatican to resign from his position as director of New Ways or be disbarred from his religious order. His response provides a perceptive reply: "When you have a fight in the family, do you leave the family?"[19]

Summary of Comparisons

The comparison of our respondents to those of the NCCB study shows some demographic differences in the age, types of communities, and affiliation reported by the gay priests, differences that may be due merely to the sampling procedure we used rather than to the real population distribution of gay priests. Distributions in residency throughout the United States and types of assignments were found to be quite similar for the two samples. Other more personal differences helped us to develop a basis for beginning to compare the sociopsychological profile (if one exists) of gay priests with that of priests in general.

The priests in our sample were found to have the same high frequency of positive spiritual experiences as the NCCB sample. The differences in the negative experiences suggests that the priests in the NCCB sample were more prone to feelings of being tempted away from God whereas our sample reported higher frequencies of feeling rejected by God.

Priests in both samples reported about the same levels of satisfaction with a variety of issues associated with their professional responsibilities as priests. The priests in our sample, however, reported deriving much more satisfaction from activities related to their personal lives; intellectual and creative activities were the most notable in this category. On the list of possible sources of problems, more gay priests reported frequent problems in all areas compared with the NCCB sample. The greatest difference was in problems with the vow of celibacy. The results show the gay priests were generally a bit happier than the priests in the NCCB sample, but members of the gay sample were about as likely as other priests to be uncertain about their future in the priesthood or to be considering leaving altogether.

Though some important differences have been discussed, there are equally important similarities to highlight. There is no evidence to suggest that homosexuality and the priesthood are mutually exclusive in the psychological sense. Gay priests might be more prone to personal problems than the "average" priest, but apparently there are also enough spiritual and other personal sources of satisfaction to provide incentive for them to continue in the active ministry. The next section will explore the more personal feelings, behaviors, and relationships reported by our survey participants in order to understand the reasons for, and the consequences of, their decision to remain in the priesthood.

Gay Priests: Attitudes and Behaviors

Although we asked a wide variety of questions of our respondents, most of our interest was in the many ways their sexuality related to their priesthood. This section will present the responses to questions that fall into four main categories: personal affect, or their feelings about homosexuality and the priesthood; personal behaviors; interpersonal relations; and estimates of the pervasiveness of homosexuality among clergymen.

The analysis in these categories will include information collected and analyzed by the Rev. Richard Wagner in his dissertation research, based on personal interviews with fifty gay priests.[20] His research was subject to the same analytic constraints as this study, because he relied on networks of personal friendships, as we did, to construct his sample rather than using random sampling techniques. However, his research does provide a much richer source of information, because his data are based on personal interviews with each of the respondents that lasted an average of ninety minutes. Many of the findings in the Wagner report will be used to add a more complete discussion to our findings.

Personal Affect

In the classic 1948 study *Sexuality and the Human Male*, Kinsey used a 7-point scale on which his subjects could indicate their subjective sexual orientation anywhere between completely heterosexual (0) to completely homosexual (6), with 3 as the midpoint between these two extremes. Most of our sample (94.6%) responded to this scale with ratings of 4, 5, or 6. Three priests placed themselves at 3 and two at 2. These five priests were among the twelve who stated their current sexual orientation as "bisexual."

Bisexual respondents were not excluded from the sample, because their sexuality includes homoeroticism and therefore, at least at times, puts them in conflict with the traditional teachings of the Church regarding homosexuality. Bisexuality may seem quite curious to the heterosexual (or homosexual) outsider, but it apparently can also be perplexing for bisexuals themselves.

I have engaged many close friends in discussion about my bisexuality—primarily trying to discover which orientation is "dominant." The orientation seems dead-center. I am curious about my own bisexuality, wondering if I am *even more* "screwed-up" than the average hetero- or homosexual?!

Although we did not receive a sufficient number of responses from bisexuals to allow for a parallel analysis of their responses throughout the study, further examination of our data revealed that the distribution of responses to the questions of interest here by these twelve priests was not notably different from that of our homosexual respondents. Their responses were therefore included with those of our gay respondents in the analysis.

A particularly delicate topic that surfaces occasionally (receiving national media coverage at times) is that of a gay priest who is attracted to adolescent boys. Such priests are in an unusually difficult situation in terms of their own sexual identity because, not only are they aware of being labeled "deviant" because of their homosexuality, they realize they run the risk of becoming virtual outcasts if they choose to act on their attractions. Two of our respondents brought up such concerns.

I feel that the very difficult and mostly neglected area of priests being attracted to young males (16–22 years [old]) has been neglected to an extent in this survey. From my present experience in counseling and dealing with priests and religious daily, this "magic age" needs lots more exploring and expertise. It is tragic that priests find themselves in the courts of law (Civil and Religious), abandoned by family and friends, living in fear and dread, wanting to be free of such attractions—with little hope of help until now—but crying out for help, understanding, and the ability to accept oneself as being no longer alone in this area! I know because I have been there (in Europe as well as the U.S.) and I meet a couple of times weekly with groups of friends and religious with similar difficulties that have never had the opportunity to really deal with [this] in any understanding and affirming manner.

I am strongly attracted to adolescents, which has been problematic in my priesthood. My current assignment . . . was recommended as safe in that I was less likely to "act out" in this setting. Other recommended settings included: teaching in a girls high school, being chaplain for retired nuns [or] at a mental institution.

With the exception of these two respondents, the self-perception of the majority of our respondents appears to be quite positive. As will be discussed in the chapter entitled "Invisible Gifts," most of these priests are glad to be gay and see it as a very special aspect of their personality.

There is little [in the questionnaire] about the homosexual spiritual life and self-image. Many of us see ourselves as having a special charism, vocation or special talents. See Richard Woods' book *Another Kind of Love*.

I truly see the "coming out" process as a spiritual awakening and a real exodus event/experience when taken in the context of my faith in the Christ event.

In terms of morality, I don't feel homosexuality is wrong or sinful. I'm happy to be gay. I can't see the acts (unless irresponsible or insensitive to others) as sinful either. Homosexuality is not a disease—it's a way of life, an orientation that some people have. It is not a choice and does not need to be changed.

There are, however, exceptions.

I am not happy about being gay, and while too active (almost addictive) I see this as a dead-end. I think gays lead a sad, sad life—full of dead-ends. They did get the shitty end of the stick when God let us loose on this earth. It's a great mystery—right after the Trinity I must put this mystery.

Our respondents were also asked to state the age at which they were first aware of the orientation they coded on the

Kinsey scale. Wagner used a slightly different approach by asking his subjects to state the age at which they first began to admit to themselves they were gay. Table 6 shows the responses in both studies to the questions on age of awareness. The two samples vary greatly on the age distributions, differences that could be due to the variant wording of the questions.

Table 6.

Age of First Awareness or Personal Admission of One's Own Homosexuality, Network and Wagner Data

AGE	Network (N = 100)	Wagner (N = 50)	Difference
Less than 10	18.0%	0.0%	18.0%
10 to 15	43.0	20.0	23.0
16 to 20	19.0	22.0	3.0
21 to 25	9.0	8.0	1.0
26 to 30	7.0	34.0	27.0
Over age 30	4.0	16.0	12.0

NOTE: Wording differed in the two studies. Network: "At what age were you first aware of this orientation?" Wagner: "At what age did you first begin to admit to yourself your gay sexuality?"

Assuming that the usual age at ordination is about 25, it appears that half of Wagner's sample were aware that they were gay prior to ordination. A much larger proportion (89%) of our sample were aware of their current sexual orientation by age 25; half were aware before the age of 15. Further analysis of our data revealed that 75.2 percent first became aware of their current sexual orientation before they entered the seminary, 19.8 percent during their seminary years, 5 percent after they were ordained. The majority of our respondents clearly made the decision to enter the seminary with already at least some awareness of their homosexuality.

Whether their decision to enter the priesthood was made in spite of this awareness or because of it cannot be determined from our data. Chapter 2 cites instances of young men interpreting their lack of attraction to females as a "sign" they were called to the religious life. However, we cannot conclude this occurs with the majority of gay males considering the priesthood. What we can assume is that the topic of sexuality was more than a casual concern for gay seminarians as they began training for the priesthood.

The process of spiritual formation required for ordination demands more of the aspirant than merely attending an accredited school and successfully completing a prescribed course of study. Seminaries are designed to train future priests through increasing levels of scholarship and restrictions on their "secular" life from the time the students enter until they are ordained. In addition, many seminaries can be considered "total institutions" in that they are self-contained environments in which contact with secular society is minimal.

We asked our respondents to rate the influence their seminary training had on their sexual attitudes using a 7-point scale from "very positive" (0) to "very negative" (6). About one-fourth of our sample (23%) gave it some sort of a positive rating; one-fourth (26%) gave it a neutral rating; and half (51%) gave it a negative rating. These findings imply a felt need by our respondents for a reevaluation of how sexuality is (and is not) dealt with in spiritual formation.

Generally perceived by gays as homophobic, the seminary setting can coerce self-denial or repression that may ultimately stimulate inappropriate "acting out."

For me, homosexuality had always been a mystery. I chose to keep it a mystery from myself and others prior to ordination. I was afraid of dealing with the issue of my orientation in the seminary because I was afraid I would not be accepted or ordained. I had many friends who were active homosexuals in the seminary process. I would listen to them, their struggles, their failures and successes and would process what all of that could possibly mean in light of my felt homosexual orientation. I simply passed it off as a "phase" I was going through. No luck; the "phase" was causing me to be seriously depressed and also in a homosexual relationship with a married man.

I often wonder if my homosexual attraction is in part pseudo because of my long-time association with males only. The law forbidding marriage made me shun close relationships with women (and men). After [some] years [on leave] I returned to the priesthood.

There is also some question about how well the current curriculum provides for a smooth and productive transition from the somewhat "controlled" environment of the seminary to the reality of independent ministry.

Shortly after ordination, I was 24 at the time, I strongly felt the need for intimacy that was not limited to sexual intimacy but did not exclude it. The seminary experience allowed the development of deep and abiding friendships with my friends who were available around the clock. After ordination, the sense of solitary living totally reversed that experience. Frequent phone calls and weekly dinners helped but did not counteract the experience of loneliness.

We found that while 70 percent of all priests responding in the NCCB survey felt that their seminary experiences prepared them well for the life of a priest, only 24.8 percent of our sample felt this way.

Another great concern for our respondents is celibacy. All Catholic priests take the vow of celibacy, which by definition means that they will not marry. This also implies that they will refrain from sexual activity; such activity outside of marriage is forbidden by the Church. Because nearly all the priests in our sample report they have engaged in sexual acts with another person at least once since they were ordained, it is important to understand their views on this subject.

Before presenting our findings, however, it may be useful to at least attempt a clarification of what celibacy is, particularly for the non-Catholic reader. It became clear to us as we presented the preliminary results of this research that many people think either that Catholic priests are somehow incapable of sexual activity or (more commonly) that for a priest to engage in sexual activity with someone else would necessarily nullify his rights and position as a priest in the Catholic church. It is perhaps better to think of a priest's commitment to celibacy (in the traditional sense) as a commitment to fidelity with the Church in much the same way as a man and a woman promise to remain faithful to each other in marriage. And just as a husband's infidelity does not automatically lead to divorce from his wife, so the sexual activity of a priest does not irrevocably negate his commitment to and his position in the Church. Given that the need for celibacy as a professional requirement has periodically been a point of some controversy in the Roman Catholic church, and that the commitment is made to an institution rather than an individual spouse, it may not appear so shocking that many of our respondents have chosen to interpret celibacy in ways other than traditional.

Table 7 presents the results of two questions related to celibacy. The first question, "How do you understand your commitment to celibacy?" allowed the respondent to indicate as many of the five possible responses as he felt applied to himself. The most common response (58.6%) was that celibacy was an ideal rather than a law that must be obeyed. Total sexual abstinence, probably the most widely accepted definition among Catholics, ranked the least common (12.1%) among these priests. That one-third of our sample reported they were uncertain about how they viewed their commitment to celibacy is perhaps the most noteworthy result of this question.

As shown in Table 4 earlier, in the area of personal problems, the largest difference between our sample and the NCCB sample of all priests was about the topic of celibacy. The uncertainty or the tendency to view the vow as not precluding sexual activity that we discovered among our respondents (see Table 7) suggests that, although these priests are attempting to resolve the dissonance between what they feel is right and what the Church says is right, celibacy is still one of the greatest sources of frustration in their lives. In spite of the frustration, there are gay priests who continue to support the requirement of celibacy.

Table 7.

Responses to Questions on Celibacy, Network Data

	Network (N=99)

"HOW DO YOU UNDERSTAND YOUR COMMITMENT TO CELIBACY?"
(Circle all that apply.)

a) It is an ideal rather than a law which must
be obeyed. — 58.6%

b) Forgo marriage but not necessarily sexual
activity. — 35.4

c) I am uncertain at this time. — 33.3

d) Attempt to avoid all acts of sexual pleasure. — 16.2

e) Total sexual abstinence as proof of my
devotion. — 12.1

"WHICH OF THE FOLLOWING BEST DESCRIBES HOW YOU DEAL WITH
CELIBACY?" (Circle only one.)

a) I consider my sexual life as separate from my
life as a priest. — 41.4%

b) I have been unable to resolve this issue. — 24.2

c) I abstain from sex with others because I choose
to do so. — 19.2

d) I abstain from sex with others because I feel
I am forced to do so. — 4.0

e) Other* — 11.1

*Responses to this question are discussed in the text.

I see celibacy as a gift which frees us to love God hopefully more as God loves us. Although I am rarely sexually active, I find celibacy to be an important part of my spiritual life.

I am a religious priest. I believe in celibacy as necessary for religious life. When, however, religious life does not live up to what was promised (e.g., supportive community when I consciously give of myself to the life of the community) I get discouraged and feel a hunger for "skin" as well as significant companionship. Sometimes this leads to sexual activity.

My notion of celibacy: my primary relationship is with the Church rather than with one other person. However, in the growth and development of my relationships, I do not exclude sexuality.

I struggle with celibacy in what I would characterize as an institutional, disciplinary way. I have no doubts that (a) homosexual activity (with the same limits as heterosexual activity) is part of God's plan, and (b) celibacy is not by divine decree but merely disciplinary. My own sense of integrity demands that my personal life correspond to my public life—that I be what I appear to be. On the other hand, celibate life, even in community and with gay friends, is hard. At one point in my life, while in graduate studies, I had a lover. Given present realities, institutional and personal, I have decided to live the ideal, but fully aware that I may not.

Further evidence of their attempt to resolve the conflict between personal institutional ideals is revealed in answers to the question regarding how these gay priests deal with celibacy. In this case, respondents were asked to choose only the one best answer of the five possible choices. The most common response (41.4%) was that they considered their sexual life separate from their life as a priest. Two-thirds of those who reported that leading a celibate life was not a significant problem were among this group who have "compartmentalized" their private lives from their priesthood.

Despite the logistical difficulties, I think celibacy should be optional for priests. The allowance of men coming into the Catholic church from the Episcopal church and being ordained married priests seems to be getting the foot in the door. I am amazed that Catholic priests are not up in arms over this. Charity should start at home!

I've come to the conviction that a diocesan priest's forced "commitment" to celibacy is not a vow in any sense of the concept, theologically . . . a promise at most. And, since it is forced, it has no moral binding power as long as scandal is avoided.

I do not know that I am all these things [gay and priest] at the same time. Letting myself be a lover in every way and understanding that in the context of priestly celibacy is a tremendous challenge. I pray each day to embrace all of who I am.

Celibacy is an ideal taught by the Church which we try to live up to with moments of success and failure. I am working on growing in this area.

I am uncomfortable labeling myself as an "active homosexual" as it is within the last year or so that I have allowed myself a dialogue with that "shadow" side of my personality. I'm not sure where this is all leading, but I am comfortable now . . . a bit more energized and far less depressed.

The next most common response on dealing with celibacy (24.2%) was uncertainty, again indicating confusion among our respondents over this issue. It should be noted that age appears to be negatively correlated with confusion over celibacy; almost half of those responding "uncertain" were under 35 years old. Only 4 percent reported that they felt "forced" to abstain from sexual activity. Of the eleven priests who chose to respond "other" to this question, most stated that they had integrated their sexual orientation into their priesthood in some successful way.

A section of Wagner's report was devoted to further clarification of the issue of celibacy. All but one of the fifty gay priests interviewed by Wagner rejected the need for mandatory celibacy. The most common theme among the many reasons given by these priests for their negative views of the vow of celibacy was the futility of attempting to mandate what they felt was a virtue. Although some felt celibacy might be an appropriate requirement for members of religious orders who have made a special commitment of service to the Church, most agreed that the ability to successfully lead a celibate life was a valuable and unique quality of gifted individuals, not something that can be required of people regardless of their desire to obey. Other reasons cited included the lack of scriptural or theological basis for the requirement of celibacy and, in the opinion of one interviewee, the general lack of adherence to the vow.

Of those gay priests in our sample who are currently sexually active, it is true that some (perhaps most) feel a certain regret about their decision to ignore their promise to remain celibate. What is most interesting is that those who wrote about their guilt never once mentioned this guilt as deriving from a sense of betrayal of their spiritual commitment to God and/or to their superiors. It resulted, rather, from their shame at giving false impressions to others who assume they are remaining celibate.

I feel somewhat guilty over my occasional sexual activity. The guilt is not about the acts but about betraying some people's expectations of how I "should" act. However, I don't think responsible sexuality conflicts with my life as a priest.

I myself find "living a lie" by being sexually active a heavy burden in conscience. Good old guilt! I *did* make the promise to be sexually abstinent and don't like hypocrisy. Yet, I like being a "hypocrite" in my sexual, private life a lot more than being a "lunatic" in my public, relational life, which is what celibacy seems to be doing to many! Couldn't the vow be an option, please? (I should say, celibacy has its "practical advantages" as a workaholic, but those are questionable in healthy human life.)

I understand my commitment to celibacy as a challenge to use my sexuality in a very creative and good way. Although I feel somewhat guilty at times, guilt can be a good tool in positive growth when used to check values. My guilt is that I don't always address the real problem, rather blame or not allow the goodness to come out.

Wagner asked specific questions directed at revealing the guilt priests might feel because their actions conflict with their vow of celibacy. Thirty of his fifty subjects reported they felt no guilt. One respondent, who reported that he had previously been "seriously suicidal" over being gay, offered the most blatant of resolutions: "There is no guilt. The Church is wrong." Others were less blunt, reporting that after much reflection (and, in many cases, therapy) they had chosen to follow their own conscience. Some expressed regret for not being able to be honest with others ("few gays in our society have the luxury of being completely honest"), and others feared the possibility of scandal if they were to be discovered.[21]

Looking at another aspect of the relationship of sexuality to the professional lives of our respondents, we asked if being a priest enhanced or inhibited their sexuality. Table 8 presents the results of this question as well as the results of an additional question asking how often their attitudes regarding their own sexuality interfered with their duties as a priest.

Table 8.

Responses to Questions Regarding the Relationship of the Priesthood and Sexuality, Network Data

	Network (N = 101)
"DOES BEING A PRIEST ENHANCE OR INHIBIT YOUR SEXUALITY?"	
Enhance	14.9%
Inhibit	39.6
Neither	40.6
Other	5.0
"HOW OFTEN DO YOU FEEL THAT YOUR ATTITUDES REGARDING YOUR OWN SEXUALITY INTERFERE WITH YOUR WORK AS A PRIEST?"	
Never	19.8
Rarely	44.6
Occasionally	27.7
Often/Always	7.9

A relatively small proportion (14.9%) of our sample indicated that their sexuality and the priesthood were complementary. For the most part, there appeared to be some tension between their sexuality and their priesthood for those who responded that it inhibited (39.6%) or both inhibited and enhanced their sexuality (5%). The majority of those who stated that it neither inhibited nor enhanced their sexuality (40.6%) were those who considered their sexual lives separate from their priesthood. Since roughly equal proportions (and mostly the same respondents) stated that their vocation inhibits their sexuality and vice versa, it cannot be concluded that either is of greater importance in understanding the strain between the two.

The final comparison in this section is of the sexual orientation of our respondents before and after their ordination into the priesthood. The decision to use the day of ordination as the dividing line was not based on any assumption that this event was or should have been any sort of "emotional watershed" with a direct influence on a priest's self-concept or sexuality. It was chosen as the one event common to all respondents during their adult lives, one that certainly will be remembered as a major life change for reasons unique to each individual.

As was discussed earlier, not all our respondents were aware of their current sexual orientation prior to their ordination, and not all consider themselves to be completely homosexual. We asked our respondents to answer the question "How would you describe your sexual orientation prior to your ordination?" and " . . . since your ordination?" A comparison of the self-reported pre- and post-ordination sexual orientation for our sample is presented in Table 9.

These results show that the largest change in orientation took place among those priests who believed they were bisexual or "other" before they were ordained (this latter category was made up primarily of those who stated that they were simply unaware of any sort of sexual orientation at that point in their lives). Some researchers argue that bisexuality is merely a "transition" stage during which a latent (though eventually dominant) homosexual orientation begins to come forth. However, there are theories emerging that seek to understand sexual self-identity as a dynamic process that emerges through one's relationships with others as opposed to a more static orientation that remains stable throughout one's adult life.[22]

Although only one of our 101 respondents reported that he had never been sexually active since his ordination, one-third (33.7%) of our sample currently consider themselves to be celibate. The next section deals with sexual activity as well as past and potential social and political involvement.

Table 9.

Self-Reported Sexual Orientation Before and Since Ordination, Network Data

	Total	Sexual Orientation Since Ordination	
		Homosexual	Bisexual
	(N = 101)		
SEXUAL ORIENTATION BEFORE ORDINATION			
Heterosexual	2.0%	2.0%	—
Homosexual	76.2	75.2	1.0
Bisexual	14.9	5.0	10.0
Other*	7.0	6.0	1.0
	100.0	88.1	11.9

NOTE: Percentages do not total to 100 percent due to rounding.
*Nearly all "other" responses were that the respondent was unaware of having any sexual orientation.

Personal Behaviors

We asked our respondents to indicate how often they had been sexually active with another person both before and since their ordination. The precoded answer categories for these questions were "never," "rarely," "occasionally," and "frequently."[23] Table 10 displays the percentages per answer for these questions along with a summary of the changes between pre- and post-ordination activity.

Nearly all of our respondents who were celibate before they were ordained now report some sexual activity, but only 9 percent of those not sexually active before ordination have shifted to frequent sexual activity since becoming a priest. The bulk of those who reported an increase in the frequency of their sexual activity changed from "never" to "rarely" or "rarely" to "occasionally." Further cross-checking of this information with the response to whether or not the respondent currently considered himself celibate revealed that none of these thirty-four celibate priests reported frequent sexual activity, but about one-fourth did report occasion.

Table 10.

Frequency of Sexual Activity Before and Since Ordination, Network Data

	Before Ordination (N = 101)	Since Ordination (N = 101)
FREQUENCY OF SEXUAL ACTIVITY		
Never	30.7%	1.0%
Rarely	23.8	25.7
Occasionally	30.7	36.6
Frequently	14.9	36.6

PERCENTAGES OF THOSE WHOSE FREQUENCY OF SEXUAL ACTIVITY CHANGED	
More sexually active now	53.5%
Same level now as before	37.6
Less sexually active now	8.9

Of the various topics written about by our respondents, comments regarding sexual activity were the most numerous. On this issue two themes that surfaced repeatedly were concerns about the morality of homosexual activity and the problems inherent in promiscuity.

I think it is important to distinguish active homosexuality in a faithful relationship to one person (lover) from promiscuous [activity]. The difference is considerable.

In my view of love as being the highest law, I see love as calling for the sexual expression when intimacy grows between two people. I also see the sexual expression as healthy and bonding activity which relieves the burden of stress and affirms the lovedness of both people. I also realize that it can cause stress if not integrated into the context of love.

Regarding "promiscuity" or being sexually active: if we have to cast in negative terms . . . so be it. Then, parallel all the recent thinking on masturbation; i.e., not being the grievous offense it was once thought to be . . . . What are two gay people doing, essentially, but indulging in mutual masturbation? The morality of the action would then depend on the motivation of the circumstances . . . not on the action itself (i.e., Is it an act of giving, an act of using, or what?).

But, to cast in terms of the positive; the longer we continue to get used to the separation of the procreative and unitive functions of our sexuality, the more we'll realize that we've got to change our thinking on the morality of the whole thing radically. The moral question will become "Why are you doing this?" the motivation will carry the morality rather than any outmoded concepts of biology or "natural law."

I have just come out of the closet regarding acceptance of my homosexuality within the last two months. At the present time, I feel sexual activity with others carries no morality with it *per se*. The "morality" involved here is the responsibility to oneself and the other person.

My own impressions of sexuality and personhood are really no different because of the priesthood. Moral behavior exists among all people so they do not destroy others or themselves. For me this is the starting point. Life choices people make are going to affect behavior but should not destroy the possibility of relationships between people. If in a relationship the two become genitally involved, they must both realistically weigh the ramifications of their actions.

In the priesthood it takes two *very* mature people to deal in a healthy manner with a system of life created in another time. In the end it comes to a choice of the greater good. I really believe that healthy human love between people is a share in God. I do not, however, see promiscuity or easy sex as having this blessing.

Although our measure of the frequency of sexual activity was somewhat vague, a clearer idea of the number of contacts this refers to can be roughly estimated by comparison with the results of the Wagner report. The members of Wagner's sample were asked to estimate the number of "same-sex contacts" per year in high school, college, and during the past year. Wagner was unclear about exactly what constitutes a same-sex contact, but it is assumed it refers to some form of intense sexual activity as opposed to rather casual contacts such as holding hands.

A comparison of the responses from Wagner's study with the responses from our own study (other than "never") suggests the following frequencies of contact for our respondents: The 25.7 percent of our sample who responded that they rarely engage in sexual activity coincides with the 30 percent of Wagner's group who averaged twelve same-sex contacts per year or fewer. The 36.6 percent who occasionally were sexually active parallels the 42 percent in Wagner's study who averaged twenty to seventy-five contacts per year. The proportion of our sample who reported frequent sexual activity (36.6%) is roughly equivalent to the 26 percent of Wagner's sample who averaged in excess of a hundred same-sex contacts per year.

The two most sexually active of Wagner's respondents reported in excess of 350 same-sex contacts per year. Such high levels of sexual activity must be understood in the context of one kind of gay male life-style. It is highly unlikely that these two priests were sexually active once or more every day. Theirs was apparently a common pattern among gay males who are very sexually active: periods of abstinence, from several days to weeks, followed by shorter periods of intense activity with a variety of partners in settings such as gay bars, bookstores, or bathhouses. For the most part, the various types of social/sexual activity reported by Wagner's subjects do not appear to differ greatly from those of the most gay men as reported by other researchers.[24] There were, however, some notable exceptions.

In comparing his results with those of Kinsey, Wagner found that an unusually large proportion of his sample (26%) did not have their first postpubertal same-sex contact until after age 24. Kinsey found that only 1.7 percent of the gay men in his sample fell into this category. Wagner found that 80 percent of the priests he interviewed stated they had (at least once) had only one sexual contact with another man compared with 93.7 percent found in the Kinsey report. There was also some evidence that the priests in Wagner's sample tended to develop longer lasting relationships with their partners than the gay men in the Kinsey study. Among the gay priests in the Wagner report, as well as in our network sample, there appears to be evidence of more concern for the development of long-term relationships with other men and less acceptance of promiscuous sexual activity than would be found in the general population of gay men.

We had also hoped to determine how likely it is that gay priests would publicly voice their opinions if given the opportunity. Since such activity is probably as much a function of personality as it is of personal conviction, it was also desirable to control for previous involvement in any sort of human rights movement. The intention was to see if only those with a history of such behavior would join an organization devoted to encouraging a more open dialogue with the hierarchy regarding sexuality and the priesthood. We therefore asked questions about how likely the respondent would be to join a sexuality discussion group as well as about past involvement in any sort of human rights organization.

The results of these two questions are presented in Table 11. Although there is a clear relationship between previous involvement in attempts at reform and the likelihood of such involvement with regard to sexuality and the clergy, there is little evidence to suggest that the great majority of gay priests are prepared to confront Church authorities with their concerns and/or grievances through formally organized channels.

We found the majority of our respondents stated they would not become actively involved in an organized effort to open dialogue with the hierarchy on the issue of sexuality, with over one-third of those who were previously politically active reporting they would probably not do so in this instance. This finding is particularly important in view of the assumption that the majority of the priests we heard from have disclosed their sexual orientation to others and have remained priests in spite of the negative attitudes toward homosexuality they face.

Table 11.

Likelihood of Joining an Organization to Discuss Sexuality, by Previous Political Activity, Network Data

	Total	Active	Supportive	No Opinion
	(N = 100)			
LIKELIHOOD OF JOINING A SEXUALITY DISCUSSION GROUP				
Would be actively involved	39.0%	29.0%	9.0%	1.0%
Would support such a group	54.0	16.0	36.0	2.0
Not certain at this time	5.0	—	3.0	2.0
Would probably not support such an organization	2.0	1.0	—	1.0
Total	100.0	46.0	48.0	6.0

The reluctance appears to be due to ambivalent or negative attitudes regarding the efficacy of such an effort. The verbatim comments of our respondents at times centered on their perception that many Church authorities (often their respective bishops and other superiors) are simply too "naive," "paranoid," or otherwise prejudiced about homosexuality to productively begin addressing the issue of gay clergy at this time.

I find the Church to be less than honest in dealing with the gay issue; e.g., refusal to admit that [there are] large numbers of gay clergy who lead double lives and [to] continue to demand celibacy of those so oriented whether or not celibacy is vowed.

Church authorities are becoming more and more homophobic; but the clergy [is] more and more homosexually active.

[The] Archbishop here is confused; caring, but taking [the] "party line." In this archdiocese, of the 20 men under 40 I only know of two straights. All the rest are gay. I know the Archbishop would [like to] wish this issue away but has lots of homophobic counsel.

I have personally suffered from the ignorance and prejudice of bishops and priests because of my sexual orientation and views. You do not include direct questions [in the questionnaire] about homophobia in the Church . . . caused, in my experience, by a large number of frightened gays in Church service. I am no longer [at my old position] because of that homophobia, but I am anxious to be of whatever help I can be to surface these issues in a spirit of Christian honesty and care.

Wagner was able to get more specific information from the priests he interviewed. He found that the majority of his sample had been active socially (78%), politically (62%), and ministerially (80%) with the gay community. However, in spite of this high level of involvement, over half of his sample (54%) felt that members of the gay community in general maintained negative attitudes regarding sexuality. This compares with the 88 percent who felt the Church's official attitude toward sexuality was negative.

Those who perceived negative attitudes in the gay community gave various reasons for their response. Some felt this group had "too many hang-ups" or unrealistic attitudes or that they conducted their lives with too little reflection on their experiences. Others were more harsh, accusing members of the gay community of lack of self-control and of behavior described as "sophomoric" and "neurotic, inhuman, and even psychotic."[25]

Criticisms of the Church's attitude stemmed from a perspective that the official teachings regarding sexuality and sexual activity are unnecessarily constrained. Whereas these men see their sexuality as a means of expressing their love for other men, they see the attitude of the Church as an unjustified attempt to stifle any and all sexual activity outside of marriage, even if the two people desiring a sexually intimate relationship are deeply in love with each other. Some expressed dismay over the apparent preoccupation of the Church with sexuality. In the words of one of Wagner's interviewees, "We [Catholics] seem to have more hang-ups about sex than we do about war and racism." In a succinct statement of his views of the current state of affairs in the Church, one of our respondents concluded: "Sum: Naive Ordinary, homophobic middle-age clergy, homosexual junior clergy. Will be interesting to watch."

Interpersonal Relations

Although we have no reason to believe that sexuality is the most overwhelming and continuous concern facing gay priests, we feel it is safe to assume that it will have some effect on their friendships and on the manner in which they counsel others. We therefore asked several questions that were intended to discover if our respondents were having difficulty relating well with others because of their sexual attraction to men.

The first set of responses we review deals with the types of people these priests have recently turned to when discussing concerns related to their sexuality. Table 12 lists the results and reveals that only a small proportion of our sample (5.9%) have not talked to anyone recently regarding this issue, yet none of these six respondents reported that his life at this time was generally unhappy. We assumed that if we had been able to realize a random sample of all gay priests the proportion who have not discussed this issue recently would have been substantially higher. As noted earlier in this report, our respondents should be considered among the more "open" of all gay priests regarding self-disclosure. We therefore have generally not heard from those who have yet to discuss their homosexuality with others.

Our survey results show that almost 90 percent of our sample have recently discussed the issue of sexuality with close male friends; slightly fewer than half with close female friends, confessors, and/or therapists; and only about one-fourth with their superiors and/or family members. With regard to self-disclosure to specific individuals, Wagner asked his respondents only if they had admitted their homosexuality to their superior or their parents. He found roughly the same proportions as in our sample: 36 percent had informed their bishop or provincial; 28 percent had told their parents.

Table 12.

*People With Whom Respondents Have Recently Discussed Concerns
Regarding Their Sexuality, Network Data*

	(N = 101)
Close Male Friend	88.1%
Close Female Friend	46.5
Confessor	44.6
Therapist	43.6
Superior	28.7
Family Member	20.8
No One Recently	5.9

NOTE: Multiple responses were allowed.

Two of these findings are worth noting. At least 43.6 percent
of our respondents have recently seen a therapist. Assuming
that this title was not often applied to a nonprofessional, such
as a friend offering advice, it appears that a large proportion of
our sample seek professional counseling. This therapy often
takes the form of support groups (both formal and informal)
with other gay priests and religious as well as individual
counseling with gay men who are or were in the religious life.
Those who wrote of their experiences in therapy reported
varying levels of success and, as a group, generally provided
more extensive comments and insights than others.

I realize that much of [what I have written] is irrelevant to your
study, but it gives me an opportunity to vent. I have quit therapy
because the therapists I have had have told me that my attitude toward
sex is neurotic: I am too hard on myself. I expect myself to be perfect in
this area, although I am not so in others.

Another major source of support for me has been a clergy-religious
support group of gay men. We meet once a month as a means of
support in sharing our lives with regard to sexuality, spirituality, and
ministry.

My therapist and spiritual director have also been instrumental in
my growth and maturing. My therapist is a gay man—former brother

and now a theologian and therapist. My spiritual director is a gay priest at a local retreat center.

I entered therapy with probably one of the best priest-psychotherapists in [the area]. He helped me to embrace who and what I am. I've been very happy, although life as a homosexual with not much Church institutional support or dialogue is and can be very painful. I've only been dealing with this issue for about a year now, so I've got much to learn about who I am as a priest, celibate (I'm not sure what that means), person, and lover of God and His people.

I have been in therapy for the past two years on a weekly basis . . . . Discipline has been my way of dealing with conflict in the past. Since that has not been working too well in the area of celibate commitment, I sought professional help.

[For four years] I was involved in bi-weekly individual therapy and for nine months in group therapy. [For two years] I was involved in monthly spiritual direction with a Jungian therapist and priest. While these experiences were enlightening and helpful in many areas of my life, my frustration over sexual intimacy, within the wider context of intimacy, continues. I am stymied by a pervasive fear of rejection and unclear about how to overcome it. However, I am determined to find a way to continue as a priest and to enter into an ongoing relationship that includes sexual intimacy.

I do feel that I lacked perspective (critical) guides along the way of my religious/priestly "formation." At [my age], can I put "toothpaste back in the tube"? My therapy allowed me to fully accept myself as homosexual—but [also] to act out in unwise and even dangerous ways.

There are a number of people "out" in my community, and this network of friends is vital. Without it I could not survive, nor would I choose to do so. My superiors have also, for the most part, been supportive. I have only had one negative experience.

I most appreciate the opportunities for informal sharing among other gay priests and religious. Here I find affirmation and a special sense of confidence and community.

It is also notable that discussion with superiors was second to last in the rank ordering of those our respondents have confided in regarding this personal issue. In terms of which group of people they would most frequently come into contact with, superiors would probably rank much nearer the top of this list. The fact that they rank second to last is evidence both of gay priests' common fear of rejection, often discussed in the written comments, and of the inability or reluctance of Church authorities to address the issue.

Our questionnaire did not include questions directed specifically at the emotional concerns associated with self-disclosure or the possibility of being discovered as a gay priest by others, though anxiety about this possibility is very common among them.

I feel the pressure of a double bind. Homosexuality is generally unacceptable in American society, especially [here], and in the Catholic church. Celibacy is also expected for priests. Add to this a seemingly growing conservative backlash in society and church, compounded by the AIDS phenomenon. I fear rejection in both arenas.

Such issues are probably better explored using Wagner's method of open-ended questions rather than the precoded answer category format we chose to use throughout our questionnaire. Wagner asked his respondents to record their thoughts on several questions dealing with disclosure and discrimination with reference to both gay and religious peers.

All of Wagner's respondents reported at least some significant degree of concern over the possibility that their sexual orientation might be discovered by other priests. Those who were most concerned reported fear of reprisal (loss of current assignment or future promotions), loss of the respect of other priests, and problems of being associated with "all the gay myths." Those who were less concerned tended to be those whose sexual identity was already known to some extent within their community. These men were primarily the ones who reported actually experiencing rejection or, in some cases, oppression by other priests.

Wagner asked similar questions about his subjects' secular gay peers to determine if "disclosure" of one's profession as a clergyman was problematic for a gay priest. Only two of his fifty respondents expressed no concern. About half of his sample stated great concern, primarily over the potential for involving the Church in a scandalous exposé as well as the potential for putting unnecessary strain on relationships with others. Those who had experienced any rejection or oppression from their gay peers among the laity because of their professional ties to the Church generally felt the cause was in some way related to the emotional immaturity of the antagonist. Wagner's findings suggest that it is almost as hard for a gay priest to disclose his profession to other gay men as it is for him to disclose his sexuality to other priests.

It was shown earlier in this report (Tables 3 and 4) that over 90 percent of our respondents reported the development of friendships as a frequent source of satisfaction. At the same time, 19 percent reported they frequently had problems developing close friendships, with an additional 22 percent occasionally having this problem. Some of the comments of our respondents dealt specifically with the problems they face, or that they observe in others, in developing close relationships.

I have often discussed friendship with many fellow priests—an issue of *great importance* with the promise of celibacy there. The suffering loneliness is serious: if friendly with a woman, there is the suspicion of an "affair"; if friendly with men, suspicion of being homosexual. Many friends who are priests feel caught in the dilemma of being left out of friendships at the intimate level as a consequence. I think it is serious enough to call for a change—some need counseling!

Because of a pervasive fear of rejection, family rooted I'm sure, I am very hesitant to initiate sexual intimacy even after a strong friendship has developed. I am a roundabout. Compounding this style is my predictably inappropriate choice of men who, while they may have become close friends, are not interested in a homosexual relationship or are too conflicted about their own orientation to become involved in depth. It seems I sabotage the opportunity from the outset.

Ten of my priest friends are gay, most willing to come out to each other. One of the major problems I have noted among them is an unwillingness to develop intimate friendships (not necessarily geni- tal/sexual) with other priests or lay persons. The self-image struggle being gay and priest is not fully faced so they live with superficial relationships, seek clandestine encounters, etc.

My struggle with intimate relationships will probably continue. I still do not see how this can be integrated with celibacy, maybe because I am not really committed to celibacy or convinced of its value, although it has a practical side. It leaves me free to hop from job to job and place to place. That might be bought at the high price of not experiencing intimacy. I'm not sure I'm convinced that celibates can expect a closer intimacy with the Lord than noncelibates . . . .

What kind of intimacy is compatible with celibacy? If I experienced enough affection would it alleviate some of my craving for sexual satisfaction? I obviously could go on and on, but it would be of no value to you or me.

In an effort to explore the possibility that sexual attraction may influence one's ability to build relationships, we asked two sets of questions dealing with the level of sexual attraction and ability to develop friendships with both men and women. Our results suggest there are very different dynamics involved in the relationships of the priests in our sample with women versus men. The first two questions asked, "How easy is it for you to develop friendships with women?" and " . . . with men?" and allowed five answer categories, which ranged from "very easy" (0) to "very difficult" (4). The second set of questions, "How would you describe your sexual attraction to women?" and " . . . to men?" had a 7-point scale for responses, ranging from "not at all attracted" (0) to "very attracted" (6). The breakdown shown in Table 13 display a condensed cross- tabulation of these questions separately for references to each sex.

Two-thirds (65.6%) of our sample report no difficulty in

Table 13.

Relationship of Sexual Attraction to the Development of Friendships with Men and Women, Network Data

(N = 101)	Sexually Attracted to Women		
	Hardly	Somewhat	Very
ABILITY TO DEVELOP CLOSE FRIENDSHIPS WITH WOMEN			
Easy	43.6%	29.7%	5.9%
So-so	7.9	6.9	—
Difficult	5.9	—	—

(N = 99)	Sexually Attracted to Men		
	Hardly	Somewhat	Very
ABILITY TO DEVELOP CLOSE FRIENDSHIPS WITH MEN			
Easy	—	7.1%	70.7%
So-so	—	4.0	15.2
Difficult	—	1.0	2.0

NOTE: Responses presented are collapsed versions of precoded answer categories. Friendship question: "Easy" = 0 and 1; "So-so" = 2; "Difficult" = 3 and 4. Attraction questions: "Hardly" = 0 and 1; "Somewhat" = 2, 3, and 4; "Very" = 5 and 6. See text for actual wording. Percentages do not add to 100 due to rounding.

dealing with either sex. The majority of these are very attracted to men and, at most, only somewhat attracted to women. The notable finding is related to those who reported some difficulty in building relationships with others. Fourteen of the twenty respondents who reported some difficulty in dealing with women also reported hardly any sexual attraction to women. Twelve of these fourteen priests reported easy development of friendships with men. Every one of our respondents who found women sexually attractive also stated that they easily developed friendships with women, suggesting that sexual attraction to women facilitates the development of friendships with them for these priests.

With respect to friendships with other men, there appears to be a reverse relationship between sexual attraction and growth of friendships. If anything, the problems our respondents had in developing friendships with other men were apparently due to sexual attraction to other men not lack of it. Seventeen of the twenty-two priests reporting some difficulty in developing friendships with other men were very homosexually attracted. Yet fourteen of this group of twenty-two also reported easy development of friendships with women. Only eight of all respondents reported some difficulty in friendship development with anyone, regardless of sex. In sum, presence or absence of sexual attraction to others may play an important role in building friendships for gay priests.

The last area to be explored in this section deals with the advice the members of our sample would give others regarding issues related to sexuality, given that all of our respondents professed sexual orientations other than heterosexual. We asked the respondent to indicate how he would most often advise other priests and religious on sexual matters using a 7-point scale ranging from "follow your own conscience" (0) to "follow Church doctrine" (6), followed by the same questions with reference to laypeople.

The cross-tabulation presented in Table 14 summarizes the responses to these two questions separately and with respect to each other. The great majority of our sample (89%) would advise priests and laypeople in the same manner, wherever that advice may fall on this "liberal" to "conservative" continuum. Only a slight majority (54%) would lean toward telling anyone to follow his or her own conscience when faced with a sexual issue. This is in contrast to the 9 percent who tend to advise that all should follow the traditional teachings of the Church. The small proportion of those who would allow less freedom of choice for laypeople than for those in the religious life (7%) is only slightly higher than for those who would be more conservative in their advice to fellow priests and religious (4%).

Table 14.

Comparison of Advice Given to Laity and to Other Priests and Religious Regarding Sexuality, Network Data

Advice to Other Priests and Religious

ADVICE TO LAYPEOPLE	Total	Conscience	Both	Doctrine
Follow own Conscience	57.0%	54.0%	2.0%	1.0%
Little of Both	32.0	5.0	26.0	1.0
Follow Church Doctrine	11.0	2.0	—	9.0
Total	100.0	61.0	28.0	11.0

NOTE: Responses are condensed versions of original 7-point scale: "Follow Conscience" = 0, 1, and 2; "Both" = 3; "Follow Church Doctrine" = 4, 5, and 6.

These results contradict the notion that gay priests are unanimously rejecting the Church's authority to teach on the issue of sexuality. Even the responses of priests who felt their sexual lives were a separate issue from their profession followed the same liberal to conservative distribution of the whole sample. In spite of the sexual orientation of our respondents, a significant proportion (about two-fifths) appear to be at least somewhat influenced by traditional Catholic teachings when offering counsel to others.

Pervasiveness of Gay Clergy

Our initial attempt to take a random sample of all Catholic priests in the United States failed, so we were unable to determine what proportion of priests are gay. In order to see if there was any significant level of agreement among gay priests regarding the pervasiveness of homosexuality among current and future Catholic clergymen, we asked our respondents to estimate the percentage of priests and seminarians in the United States they felt had a homosexual orientation. The results of these questions, presented in Table 15, reveal that our respondents estimate the average to be 48.5 percent of the priests and 55.1 percent of the seminarians.

Table 15.

Mean Respondent Estimates of the Percentage of Priests and Seminarians Who Are Homosexual, Network Data

| | Estimated Percentage Homosexual | | | |
| | Priests | | Seminarians | |
	Mean	SD	Mean	SD
OVERALL AVERAGE (N=101)	48.5%	13.5	55.1%	14.3
AVERAGE BY YEAR RESPONDENT WAS ORDAINED				
1960 or Before (N=12)	44.5%	17.2	50.9%	16.5
1961–1965 (N=14)	43.2	9.0	50.0	10.9
1966–1970 (N=13)	44.6	13.1	47.9	16.1
1971–1975 (N=20)	48.9	15.2	54.5	16.1
1976–1980 (N=31)	51.8	14.8	57.2	15.5
1981–1984 (N=11)	54.0	8.1	70.5	6.2

NOTE: SD = the standard deviation of the estimates.

Although these personal estimates ranged from 10 percent to 85 percent for priests and 10 percent to 95 percent for seminarians, the distributions were quite clustered around the means. Two-thirds of our sample estimated between 40 percent and 60 percent of the ordained clergy are gay (less than one-fourth of the estimates were below 40%). Three-fourths of our sample estimated between 40 percent and 70 percent of current seminarians are gay (less than 10% of the estimates were below 40%). Note that the perceived proportion of gay priests and seminarians is highest among those gay priests who have been most recently ordained. What is quite clear is that the highest percentage estimates of gay seminarians, 70.5 percent, is given by those who have most recently attended the seminary.

It must be emphasized that these estimates are based solely

on the impressions of the gay priests in our sample. Given the current lack of information on this subject, there is no way of verifying their validity. Several reviewers of this report have offered suggestions that cast doubt on the legitimacy of these estimates; others' comments lend support.

On the one hand, these estimates may be "wishful thinking" on the part of our respondents. Because of their sexual orientation and their inability to openly profess their homosexuality they be more prone to interpret or "read into" the ambiguous behavior or comments of other priests an indication that they too are gay. After many such experiences a gay priest may conclude, however correctly or incorrectly, that a significant proportion of all priests he has come into contact with are gay, even if only a small proportion of his religious peers have actually disclosed to him that they are in fact gay.

Their perception that such a high proportion of priests and seminarians are gay seems at odds with the great reluctance expressed by many of these priests to disclose their sexual orientation to other priests. If there is actually a 50-percent chance that the potential "confidant" is also gay, the fear of rejection and sense of isolation seems to be much greater than one would expect. This contradiction could be explained, however, if most of these priests felt the potential harm from an unsympathetic listener would be far greater than the potential gain from a sympathetic reaction.

Another point was raised regarding the apparent contradiction between the large estimates of gay priests reported and the rather modest rate of response to our survey. If half of the nearly fifty-nine thousand priests in the United States are in fact gay it would seem unlikely that after several waves of distributing close to two hundred questionnaires over a period of ten months we should have received only about a hundred responses. The implication of this viewpoint is that the low response rate indicates that there could not actually be over twenty-nine thousand gay priests in the United States.

It can also be argued, however, that gay priests are in the best position to give a good estimate of how many of their fellow Catholic clergymen are gay. Many priests live in residences with other priests, particularly in religious orders. Such living arrangements would be quite conducive to the kinds of personal discussions that would result in mutual self-disclosure. Theirs is also a highly mobile profession. Over 75 percent of our respondents report being at their current assignment less than five years, which suggests their assessment of the pervasiveness of homosexuality among clergymen is not necessarily based only on a particular geographical area or group of friends. The relatively recent growth of such gay Catholic organizations as Dignity and New Ways Ministry has also offered gay priests new avenues with which to develop a wide network of acquaintances with other gay priests and religious.

When asked to explain the low response rate to our survey, two of the gay priests involved in this project gave one succinct reason: fear. An acquaintance attended a Dignity conference recently and mentioned to a group of gay priests that he was aware of a study involving a survey of gay Catholic clergy. It was apparently the consensus of the group that such a study as ours was ill-advised and even potentially dangerous. They saw great possibility for public scandal and for negative action to be taken by Church authorities toward priests who are even suspected of being gay.

We were not insensitive to these concerns. Our decision to pursue the study to completion was based on the fact that we received no correspondence from anyone contacted during the data collection process requesting that we discontinue our efforts. On the contrary, many of the questionnaires returned to us included notes thanking us for our concern and wishing us well in our work. Yet, it appears that nonresponse could have been motivated, perhaps to a large degree, by the perception that publication of the results in an inappropriate manner could bring more harm than good to gay clergymen and to the Catholic church as a whole.

One final comment in support of these high estimates of the

proportion of gay priests and seminarians relates to the requirements of the profession itself. No priest is allowed to marry, which immediately rules out the substantial majority of Catholic heterosexual males who have a strong desire to marry and raise children. In contrast, the prohibition of marriage is a "nonissue" with gay males.

We found no evidence in our research or in the Wagner report to suggest that gay Catholic men are attracted to the religious life because of the likelihood of living in community with other men. On the contrary, the gay priests in both studies report a great deal of apprehension about the possibility of their sexual orientation being discovered by other priests. The decision to become and remain a priest appears to be much more a matter of their psychological convictions and spiritual devotion to the service of the Church. Until further research provides more adequate information on this issue, the estimates given by our respondents can be considered suggestive but, unfortunately, not easily verifiable.

Summary

Although the nature of our sample prohibits our making any definitive conclusions about the situation of gay clergymen in the Roman Catholic church, the results have identified several important issues, which should be of assistance if further research in this area continues. These results are particularly significant because our respondents are mainly those gay priests who have accepted their homosexuality as a positive aspect of their personality, have disclosed this identity to others, and have remained in the priesthood in spite of the frustrations they face.

Perhaps the most important finding is that homosexuality is not necessarily incompatible with the priesthood. The spiritual lives of the priests in our sample, as well as their satisfaction with their professional responsibilities, was not found to be dramatically different from that of priests in general. They are generally quite happy and do not appear to be any more likely to be considering leaving the priesthood than priests in the NCCB sample.

In contrast to the "average" priest, however, our respondents seem to have developed a more personally defined spirituality with regard to sexuality in the near absence of any official discussion of this issue as it relates to the clergy. Many of these priests have gone beyond a stage of merely questioning the Church's authority in requiring the vow of celibacy to a point where they have managed to compartmentalize their sexual lives from their lives as priests. A good number of them (particularly among the younger priests) express confusion about how they now understand celibacy in view of their current beliefs and activities.

This personal decision to reassess their vow of celibacy appears to coincide with their attitudes regarding sexuality in general. The majority feel others should follow their conscience when problems arise regarding sexuality. Nearly all of the priests in our survey have been sexually active at least once since they were ordained, and much of their private lives, sexual and social, have remained clandestine. In spite of their constrained life-styles, however, less than 40 percent indicated they would become actively involved in an organized attempt to open a dialogue between priests and the hierarchy of the Church on the issue of sexuality and the priesthood.

The findings of this study bring up many questions about past and future development of the Catholic clergy and the Roman Catholic church as a whole. We now turn to a discussion of some of the implications of the broad array of issues that have been explored.

Institutional and Interpersonal Implications

The issue of gay clergymen in the Roman Catholic church is clearly complex. The interwoven social, psychological, and theological dynamics can easily confound and constrain most attempts to arrive at satisfactory answers to questions raised in any one of these domains. In an effort to clarify some of the more important issues raised in this chapter, the institutional matters will be addressed separately from the more particular concerns related to interpersonal relations. Direct assessment of moral theology is not within our scope. It is hoped, however, that these findings will be of use to those who are qualified to undertake such a task.

Institutional Strain

No accusation can be made that the Catholic church supports an overt policy of discrimination against gay people because of their sexuality. Pope John Paul II has made it clear that a homosexual orientation is not grounds for denying anyone his or her right to be accepted. Yet given the current level of cultural and theological controversy over the issue of homosexuality within the Church, it is safe to assume that verification of the existence of gay priests will be perceived by many Catholics as a threat to the stability of the Church. As with many other forms of prejudice, this perceived threat to stability will be compounded by the lack of information on the very subject of concern. The implications of this prejudice are as numerous as its causes.

In his classic 1954 work *The Nature of Prejudice*, G. W. Allport provided many insights into the social and psychological causes and consequences of this particular form of intolerance. For this reason, we will use his work as a template to explore the issues we have brought forth in this chapter. Allport's distinction between prejudice and discrimination is of particular importance in understanding the case of the gay priest. Prejudice refers to the belief systems that emerge to support more enduring attitudes toward a particular topic. These belief systems can then be translated into action of varying intensity, including discrimination. In this view, prejudice is therefore an attitudinal cause; discrimination is the behavioral consequence.

In the case of negative prejudice toward gay priests within the religious community, these actions can take the mild form of vocalizations, such as insults or the spread of gossip. The most intense results of prejudice mentioned by our respondents were discriminatory sanctions that might take the form of unequal opportunity for advancement within the hierarchy or removal from one's current position. Allport's highest level of prejudice in action refers to acts of violence, a highly unlikely outcome in this particular situation.

The problem faced by gay priests, and the Church as a whole, is therefore understood as not being rooted in the actual or anticipated discrimination against gay people by Catholics but rather in the negative prejudice against them that has been perpetuated over the centuries to the point that it has become an integral part of the "Catholic attitude" about sexuality. It need not be emphasized that this intolerance of homosexuality coincided with contemporary public opinion and is not unique to Catholicism. However, it does seem ironic that the cultural and theological justifications that have been used to fortify the more ephemeral skepticism and confusion about homosexuality are in direct contradiction to the Christian doctrine of unqualified love and acceptance of others. This type of contradiction can only serve to undermine the legitimacy of the Church's authority to provide spiritual leadership, particularly in the minds of those who feel it is the responsibility of Church authorities to suppress this type of prejudice rather than allow it to endure.

Of the ten sociocultural determinants of prejudice identified by Allport, five are of particular relevance to our study. Those that are not discussed here are related to economic, geographic, and judicial concerns. Rapid social change (such as the "sexual revolution" in the United States during the 1960s and 1970s) and the resulting sense of normlessness (commonly referred to in the social sciences as *anomie*) is one precondition of prejudice. Such a situation forces those affected to regain their sense of order by relying on whatever information or commonly held beliefs seem to make sense. Quite often little attention is given to whether or not the information is valid or the beliefs justified. The primary concern is to arrive at a satisfactory answer to the many questions that arise during times of rapid change. Once a general sense of order is restored, there is little incentive to examine the validity of the conclusions; to do so would be to jeopardize the regained stability of the belief system.

Lack of adequate knowledge is another of Allport's conditions of prejudice, because, especially in times of rapid change, common beliefs, which are often founded on myths or rumors, are used as an inadequate substitute for fact. Ignorance is caused by barriers to communication. These barriers exist either because of a genuine lack of available facts or because of a prejudicial attitude that discourages the acceptance of the correct information. Much research is still needed into the true causes and consequences of sexuality, but we must also assume that there are many who are unwilling to accept information that would suggest that homosexuality is a legitimate and fulfilling sexual orientation.

The existence of realistic conflict is a third precursor to prejudice. For our purposes, the conflict is not to be found in violence but rather in the conflict of two ideologies: that of Church tradition versus that of the gay community. The leaders of each group are convinced of the appropriateness of their respective viewpoints and of the value of their respective constituencies. The problem of resolving this ideological conflict is compounded by the highly emotional nature of attitudes toward nearly any issue related to such an intimate topic as sexuality.

Those priests who have willingly accepted their homosexuality feel their sexual orientation is a productive and integral part of their being. They feel they could no more deny their feelings than heterosexual priests could reject their love for and attraction to members of the opposite sex. If gay leaders were to attempt a resolution with Church officials that in any way compromises the beliefs of homosexuals, these leaders would most likely be accused by some of their constituency of "caving in" under the weight of Church authority.

A similar fate is likely to be faced by Church officials who might be willing to confront tradition and begin a campaign toward more compassionate acceptance of gay people into the mainstream of Catholic culture. Many Catholics, clergy and laity alike, remain steadfast in their belief that it is valid to selectively accept or reject as appropriate the sexual behavior and feelings of others. As long as the debate remains dead-locked in a contest of opinions, ideological conflict will continue to threaten the internal harmony of the Church

The last two of Allport's conditions that create an environ-ment conducive to prejudice are both related to the mainte-nance of beliefs: myths or traditions that sustain hostility, and reluctance to accept "outsiders" or allow diversity within the group. The myths surrounding the activities of gay men are quite numerous and serve to strengthen the belief that homo-sexuality is immoral. Tales of unbridled promiscuity, pedophi-lia, sadomasochism, orgies, and other forms of "bizarre" sex rituals and fetishes combine with reports of rape and seduction to create an image of gay male sexuality as unquestionably immoral. The simple fact that nongay men (and women) also engage in these activities has clearly not led to an equally emotional rejection of heterosexuality.

The matter of assimilating "outsiders" into a traditional institution such as the Catholic church is one of great concern to our research, particularly since members of the "out-group" are already professing their membership in the Church to the extent that they have devoted themselves to the religious life.

The existence of a gay clergy presents officials of the Roman Catholic church with a perplexing dilemma. To openly promote acceptance of gays as equals in the Church invites the rage of those Catholics who have found theological and cultural justification for their condemnation. For Church officials to openly condemn the homosexual activity invites the fury of those who have found theological and personal justification for acceptance. To remain silent on the subject is to fail in their obligation as leaders of the Church to provide spiritual direction for the clergy and congregation in times of confusion. The problem takes on added dimensions in view of the cultural diversity of the worldwide congregation of Catholics and the varying levels of tolerance toward homosexuality found in different societies.

The conditions of prejudice just outlined are applicable to a wide variety of situations within any social institution. There is no compelling reason to believe that the Church should be immune to these conditions. It has been over a decade since papal endorsement of the statement by the American bishops accepting gays and denouncing their form of sexual expression. Recent Vatican proclamations accusing spiritual leaders of the Church (particularly in the United States) of permitting excessive tolerance of the gay community indicates this acceptance is far from "unqualified." Though the emergence and growth of gay rights organizations within the Church throughout this period might appear evidence of official tolerance of their cause, the growth in tolerance of American Catholics toward homosexuals and their activities has been less than dramatic. Although there is no evidence to suggest an imminent and divisive confrontation will soon occur over this subject within the Church, it would seem that a call for order would be justified. How the hierarchy of the Church chooses to respond to that call will most likely have lasting consequences.

Interpersonal Discord

In a modified sense of the term, gay priests are *marginal men*. In the social sciences this phrase is commonly used in reference to individuals or groups who are physically close to other members of the large society yet culturally remote.[26] Quite often it is these very "marginal" members of a society who are most able to "remove" themselves from their social environment and provide unique insights into the communal life that others are unwilling or unable to see. Though hardly the impartial "strangers in a strange land," these priests reveal very important aspects of their lives only with the utmost caution. It appears that they hold strong personal allegiances to both the Catholic church and the gay community, yet they are quite unwilling to openly and simultaneously identify themselves with both groups for fear of rejection. When acting as a priest, they must carefully hide all vestiges of homosexuality. When participating in the activities of the gay community, they can almost never wear the Roman collar. It is only in those relatively rare situations in which the gay priest can engage in active ministry to other gay Catholics that he can enjoy the highest level of personal fulfillment.

This situation of belonging to "dual reference groups" should not be confused with the notion of cognitive dissonance in the sense of being unable to resolve the conflicting ideologies of the two groups. Except for the issue of sexual orientation, the comparison of the NCCB survey with our data found little evidence to prove gay priests to be dramatically different from priests in general either psychologically or in their relationships with others. Evidence was also reviewed that suggests our respondents are regularly associating with other gays within and outside of the Church. These priests have accepted and remain loyal to what is good about each of the groups in conflict; this is clearly not a case of "either-or."

Perhaps the most important finding of our study is the rejection by many of our respondents of the legitimacy of Church authority regarding sexuality. Many have cognitively compartmentalized their sexual life from their life as a priest. Almost as many are uncertain how they should understand their commitment to the vow of celibacy. It is also common for them to advise others to follow their own conscience as opposed to Church doctrine when providing counsel regarding sexual matters. It would appear that the communication barriers between these priests and their superiors have led to a more personalized resolution of the conflicts in ideology.

The resentment felt by gay priests toward their superiors, either because of the latter's active discrimination or their passive neglect to address the problem of prejudice, has apparently resulted in the emergence of small clandestine support groups. Discordant ideologies commonly lead to formation of clearly defined institutional boundaries.[27] That we find little evidence of a possible coalition developing, or even the desire for one, is likely to be explained by concern about the possibility of reprisals combined with gay priests' sense of commitment to their profession. Coalition formation is also greatly constrained by the high level of geographic mobility of these priests.

Given that any organized religion is by definition a moral institution, it would be wholly unacceptable for the Roman Catholic church in contemporary society to openly promote a policy of active discrimination against homosexuals. However, since the Church has not taken a more active stand in obstructing prejudice against gay people, our respondents appear to be experiencing the effects of a more nebulous form of passive discrimination. They are unlikely to disclose their sexual orientation to others not only out of fear of personal rejection by that individual but also of future consequences that information could have on their career within the Church. At the present time, members of the hierarchy need not explain why a priest was either passed over for promotion or suddenly reassigned to another position elsewhere. With some restrictions, the decision of a bishop or major superior in such matters is usually final.

Our respondents are indeed committed to their homosexual identity, but they are also committed to their role as priest. Few of them stated that they are considering leaving the priesthood. Written comments suggest that they would do so only if they were certain that to remain would ensure a constant struggle with others. They find a great deal of personal fulfillment in carrying out the responsibilities of the priesthood and in the working and social relationships they have developed with other people. Thus, they maintain their allegiance to the Catholic church in spite of the rather antagonistic attitudes toward homosexuality they confront.

There is evidence to suggest that psychological maladjustments that result from prejudice are probably more a function of the *anticipation* of discrimination than the actual experience of an overt act of discrimination. A multinational study of gay men found strong positive relationships between anxiety over societal reaction to the respondents' sexual orientation and a wide variety of psychological maladjustments, including low self-acceptance, depression, interpersonal awkwardness, and low faith in others.[28] This anxiety over *potential* antagonism was higher in the United States than in Europe, but on neither continent did psychological maladjustment appear to have any relation to having actually experienced hostility. Recent research supports the hypothesis that anticipation of a hostile social environment is a more significant determinant of psychological problems for gay men than actually experiencing prejudice.[29] In view of these findings, the gay priest is considered to be in a rather high risk group because of his commitment to the Church and to his own self-identity.

In order to understand the consequences of trying to balance these dual allegiances, Allport again provides a useful outline. In his chapter entitled "The Traits of Victimization," he discusses the psychological and interpersonal characteristics developed by those who are the victims of prejudicial environments. These traits fall into two major categories: those related to people who feel the prejudice is unfounded (the majority of the priests in our sample, for example) and those related to people who feel others are justified in their negative attitudes (gay priests who cannot accept their own homosexual orientation). These two groups of characteristics are not intended to be mutually exclusive. They are merely presented as such to provide a means of understanding two significant classifications of gay priests: those who were likely to respond to our survey, and those who were not.

As shown in the analysis of our survey results, the majority of our respondents self-identify as gay and accept that orientation as an important and productive component of their personalities. In trying to resolve the frustration they feel as gay men and Catholic priests they have decided to follow their conscience and hope for change. Two of the traits identified by Allport, "the strengthening of in-group ties" and "clandestine behavior," were the most commonly mentioned in the written comments we received. The possibility of rejection combined with the generally perceived threat to reputation and career reinforce the need to maintain alliances with other gay people, gay priests whenever possible. The nature of such friendships would hardly be a topic for open discussion within the religious community.

Two more traits of victimization noted by Allport are "prejudice against others" and "obsessive concern or suspicion." The idea here is that "prejudice begets prejudice," even within the realm of the Catholic clergy. Some of our respondents were sympathetic toward the dilemma faced by the bishops and superiors of the Church, but many more were angered by what might be considered a "convenient hypocrisy" of silence or conservative politics. We cannot ascertain whether our respondents were "obsessively" concerned or suspicious, but the tone of the general comments regarding the negative attitudes of "the Church" would suggest this may also be true.

"Enhanced striving" and "militancy" are the last two of Allport's traits of victimization that might well be applicable to gay priests. It seems likely that a man who has accepted the fact that he is gay and has committed himself to the religious life would have an added incentive to push his abilities to the limit. To his fellow priests who know he is gay, he would be proof that gay men can be successful in the priesthood; to his gay peers who know he is a priest, he would be proof that homosexuality and spirituality need not only coexist but also can actually complement one another. However, should this desire for success be met with resistance, personal or institutional, it is also likely that the aggressively oriented priest would choose to publicly confront Church officials. Given the reported reluctance of our respondents to become actively involved in an organized attempt to open a dialogue with the hierarchy on the issue of sexuality and the priesthood, it appears such aggressive acts of militancy by priests will probably remain isolated in the near future.

As was stressed at the beginning of the chapter, our sample represents only a subset of gay priests. They identify themselves as gay and, for the most part, accept their homosexuality as good in spite of the social problems associated with being identified as such. We assume that there are also priests who are unwilling, or unable, to accept their homosexual orientation. Although a thorough examination of the effects of this type of self-denial is outside the scope of this report, Allport's characteristics of people who are the victims of prejudice and accept it as justified provides a useful guide to creating working hypotheses about these particular priests.

The self-denying gay priest who regularly feels strong sexual attraction to other men is likely to develop a variety of behaviors and attitudes that will only accentuate the anxiety he is trying to mask. It need not be stressed that the psychological depression resulting from this self-denying behavior can only serve to obstruct the full potential for interpersonal relations, which are an integral part of the role of priest.

Allport also discussed "in-group aggression" and "symbolic status striving" as consequences of accepting the attitudes of the majority in spite of one's own feelings. A self-denying gay priest might direct antagonistic remarks against homosexuality in an attempt to prove to others that he is "above reproach." Further attempts to prove this could lead to an effort to project an extremely righteous and devout image. Obsessive biblical scholarship, strict adherence to rules of self-sacrifice, and public involvement in numerous charitable activities would be some examples of this behavior. Of course, this is not to imply that any priest who engages in these types of behavior is a hypocrite. We only suggest that the self-denying gay priest may feel forced to these activities in an effort to conceal feelings he has defined as unacceptable.

The last three conditions identified by Allport are related to the psychological consequences of trying to resolve cognitive dissonance by defining one's feelings as wrong: "withdrawal and passivity," "self-hate," and "neuroticism." Even if he is heavily involved in symbolic status striving, the personal feelings and emotions of the self-denying gay priest may be carefully concealed from even his closest friends. He is likely to be secretive about his private life and take on an air of indifference when others try to learn more about him. Denying his intense feelings of homosexuality over long periods of time could manifest itself in psychological pathologies that, in some cases, could have severe consequences.

These speculations based on Allport's research, relating to both "self-accepting"and "self-denying" gay priests, are in no way intended to be understood as inevitable consequences of the current prejudice against homosexuality within the Church. The infinite variety of the human experience is the ultimate determinant of how people will react in a given situation. There is, however, strong reason to believe that the active and passive forms of discrimination within the Church will constrain attempts to fortify its social stability and integrity as a moral institution.

As with most attempts to explore relatively "uncharted waters," this report is likely to generate more questions than answers. It is hoped that the information provided here will be of use in clarifying what kinds of questions should be addressed in the future.

The questions raised here that are likely to be most controversial are those regarding celibacy, the relationship of the priest to his superiors, the spiritual guidance priests provide to others, and the possible discrepancy between personal activities and public "presentation of self." The fact that the gay priests in our sample appear to be following a more "personalized" spirituality instead of the more traditional mandates for the priesthood has important sociological and theological implications for further research and discussion on the structure of the Catholic church.

On the issue of sexuality in general, it seems that much work could be done to understand the role of celibacy in the life of a priest or religious and how they compensate for their inability to be "legitimately" sexually active. The psychological impact of striving for a life void of such activity may have damaging effects on the behavior of those who might otherwise be enthusiastic and productive servants of the Church. Further study could address the process of how open discussion of sexuality and the celibate life is dealt with in seminaries, convents, and other formation environments.

Until further research can be undertaken, there is a still more immediate concern: what (if anything) should be done at present by those members of the Church who are concerned about the issues of homosexuality among Catholics in general and among priests and religious in particular. Chapter 5 will conclude with specific suggestions that could be of use to anyone willing to accept the task of creating a forum for productive discussion of the issues raised here.

The collection of essays entitled *Lesbian Nuns: Breaking Silence* attracted considerable attention and was even banned by some Catholic groups before its contents were disclosed. There was apparently no official reaction to the book by Church leaders, presumably because only nine of the fifty-one contributors were still active members of religious orders and thus there was no compelling reason for Church officials to once again subject themselves to open challenge. The results of our survey, though in many ways reiterating the concerns expressed by the authors of *Lesbian Nuns*, give evidence that gay religious do not necessarily leave when they cannot find acceptance; the great majority of our respondents appear to have every intention of remaining in the priesthood. As long as they do, they will most likely remain a constant yet relatively quiet reminder to the Catholic hierarchy of the challenge they face regarding the legitimacy of their authority over sexual morality.

II. PERSONAL REFLECTIONS

2. Invisible Gifts: The Experience of Gay Priests

REV. R. EDWARDS

There's a well-known scene at the end of the movie *La Cage Aux Folles* in which a priest officiating at a marriage turns a page of a book with an exaggerated, effeminate gesture. The gesture brings the movie, which deals good-naturedly with the love life of an aging homosexual couple, to a humorous end, but it also suggests the existence of homosexuality among the clergy.

Though there certainly are gay priests and religious, that final scene in *La Cage* is a caricature and hardly describes the totality of the experience—or the appearance—of gay priests. Popular opinion often limits male homosexuality to obviously effeminate behavior, but the gay male experience is much wider. The same may be said for gay male priests: a few may be identifiable on the basis of mannerisms, but most are not.

This chapter will attempt to describe the gay priest, who is often invisible, in more detail, and will do so by asking several questions. First, how are priests gay? That is, what form does homosexuality take among the clergy? This is an important question, since it is often assumed that if one is celibate one has no sexuality. That is not true, and sexuality, for gay priests as well as for heterosexual ones, is an important part of their identity and therefore of their priesthood. Second, what are the consequences for a priest who has recognized his gay sexuality after ordination, or even during or before seminary training?

Rev. R. Edwards is the pseudonym of a gay priest.

79

We often assume, on the one hand, that gayness is the result of a perverse and sinful choice, or, on the other hand, that someone is "born with it"; in fact, neither is quite true, and the process of acknowledging one's gayness (or "coming out") is important. Third, how can gayness be seen as a grace—both for the church and for the individual gay priest?

There are a number of reasons why a discussion of these issues is necessary. First among them is that there are lots of gay priests; this fact has not been scientifically verified, but my own experience and that of many others suggests that at least half of American priests are "gay" in one of the ways I will describe below, and I have no reason to think that the figure is lower in other countries. Second, although a number of church documents address the question of pastoral care for gay Catholics, none of them, in my estimation, does so adequately. While they encourage compassion and understanding for the homosexual, the vigor with which they reaffirm the traditional teaching (which finds homosexual acts to be intrinsically evil) often speaks louder than admonitions to acceptance of and respect for the gay person. In fact, I doubt that most Catholics know that even the most conservative Church documents make a fundamental distinction between the person who is homosexually oriented, and in no way sinful or inferior because of that, and homosexual acts, which are the focus of the moral debate. In the end this is probably an incoherent distinction (since I doubt if we can legitimately distinguish who a person is sexually from what a person does sexually), but it is crucial that Christians at least acknowledge the basic goodness of homosexual persons, even if they have questions about what they do in bed.

And if these Church documents are too brief and too general to be of much help in counseling the lay Catholic gay person, they say nothing at all about gay priests and religious, who, because of their public commitment to celibacy, constitute a special case. The topic of gay priests and religious deserves attention not only because priests and religious are Catholics, and therefore have a right to the Church's pastoral care, but also because there is a certain unhealthy duplicity possible in a Church that denies the legitimacy of homosexual acts, barely acknowledges the dignity and place of homosexual persons, yet has large numbers of gay clergy. I wouldn't characterize this as hypocrisy (though many others have) because I don't doubt the sincerity of our Church leaders; I believe they are really trying to uphold morality. Still, certain incidents, such as Archbishop O'Connor's reluctance to comply with the terms of a New York City antidiscrimination ordinance in the hiring of homosexuals, among other more recent examples, make the inconsistency stand out and, understandably, alienate large numbers of gay Catholics who know priests who are gay but afraid to speak out. (I hasten to point out that I do not advocate publicly proclaiming one's sexual preference, particularly if one is celibate; however, there are times when perhaps it is necessary to do so in the interest of integrity.)

Finally, this chapter is necessary to help the Church (and gay priests themselves) acknowledge the gifts gay clergymen bring to ministry. For too long we have seen gayness as a form of stunted development that causes scandal and impedes ministry. I believe that just the opposite is true. Gayness is another, albeit statistically abnormal, form of sexual development. It does not necessarily reflect emotional immaturity or sickness, and it carries its own gifts, abilities, and benefits. I could recite a list of well-known historical figures who were giants in their fields and whose gayness did not impede their talent or their contribution to society; I could recite a list of less well-known but equally talented priests who are gay and who have been eminently successful in their work. That success—and sanctity—are not in spite of their gayness but within it, and probably because of it. The primary presupposition I make here, then, is that gayness is not a disability that must be overcome, but a gift, a special way of relating to the world that must be acknowledged and respected where it occurs. Many fear that such an acknowledgment will lead to widespread homosexuality and even abandonment of normal sexual relations. That is an ungrounded fear. Gayness has always been a statistical abnormality, occurring in only a small percentage of the population. I know of no evidence that acceptance increases incidence, nor that acceptance poses any threat to society. I can see no reason why acceptance of gayness among the clergy poses any threat to the Church.

I do not speak as a professional therapist, though I do hold postgraduate degrees in theology. I speak as a gay priest who has thought and prayed about his gayness for fifteen years, and who has found his gayness to aid his ministry, his spiritual life, and his personal relationships. Gayness is a part of who I am, and I believe that being gay, though at times a trial, has far more often been a joy and a sign of God's grace.

I will avoid the use of the word *homosexual* because its connotations seem too harshly critical for this context and it seems to focus inordinate attention upon genital activity, which is only a small part of homosexuality, especially for celibates. I prefer the use of the word *gay*, which though of rather recent origin and of dubious accuracy, at least suggests that there is more to the homosexual experience than sex.

In addition, because I am a male and have spent a third of my life in a male religious community, my reflections will derive from that experience. I do not purposely exclude the experience of women religious, but simply do not feel competent to speak about it.

Varieties of Clerical Gayness

What do I mean by "gay priests"? There is no simple answer to this question. We could say that gay means, among other things, "sexual and emotional attraction to a person of the same sex," but there are dozens of distinct ways in which this is manifest. At the very least, however, let me say that my subject is those priests and religious who are constitutionally homosexual—that is, those who, whether they are aware of it or not, are primarily attracted to people of the same sex. If we use the "spectrum" analysis of sexuality (a scale of one to six in which one is complete heterosexuality and six complete homosexuality), this discussion is limited to those who are mostly homosexual in orientation—a three or better. I do believe there are people who are truly bisexual or perhaps undecided, but they are few and far between. The vast majority of us are decidedly straight or gay, and that from a very early age. For most of us, the only decision we have to make is whether we are willing to acknowledge our sexual identity; it is rarely a question of perverse "decision" to be gay. In fact, quite the contrary is the case. Most of the gay priests I have known have gone through lengthy, agonizing struggles with their gay sexuality and only come to accept it with difficulty. As one gay friend of mine quipped, "Choose to be gay! My God, who would choose all this misery?" The misery is not so much in being gay as it is in not being like others and having to bargain for acceptance and self-esteem, always feeling one is on the brink and could be rejected at any moment. Eventually, however, most gay people (I include myself) come to a genuine appreciation of their gayness; they come to see that like any other dimension of personality, it has its advantages and that the distinctive perspective it affords can be a real gift. I will discuss the "gift" of being gay in further detail shortly.

More specifically, then, we might divide gay priests and religious into three general categories: those whose attitude toward their sexuality is one of denial; those whose attitude is one of qualified acceptance, either intrapersonal or interpersonal; and those who fully accept that they are gay, intrapersonally, interpersonally and socially. Within these three general categories, however, there are numerous subdivisions. Let us turn to those who, though objectively gay, deny that fact.

Denial

Since Shakespeare ("The lady doth protest too much, me-thinks," *Hamlet*, III, ii) the word *denial* has become a heavy one; we speak of the "denial" of death, the "denial" of painful reality, the "denial" of the inevitable, the "denial" of sexuality, but in each case it is a question of an unconscious refusal to deal with some fact. Gays are particularly sensitive to other gay people who are "into denial," or who are "in the closet," as they often say, and readily speculate about "who is and who isn't" gay. The fact is, there are lots of people who are, but who wish they weren't and who try to conceal the fact in one way or another.

Generally, there are what we might call "benign" denial and "hostile" denial. Into the former group fall people like a friend of mine who throughout his seminary years knew that there were gay people, and even had a number of male sexual partners himself, yet never saw himself as gay. When a friend of his confided that he was gay, my friend even nodded understandingly, and pledged his continued friendship, but never once thought that he was in the same boat. Only years later, shortly before ordination, did he realize what his more youthful sexual experiences meant.

Another friend, who was a member of a religious order for more than twenty years, and who, during that time, had an ongoing (but clandestine) sexual relationship with another man that lasted several years, was never able to admit he was gay. "Gay people," he said, "are narcissistic and hang around those sleazy bars." Reducing the definition of gay to fit his needs, he was able to forestall acknowledgment of his own sexuality. When he was nearly forty years old, sudden realization of his emotional needs forced him to admit he could never muster sufficient sexual attraction to a woman to marry one.

Still another form of benign denial is a kind of sublimation of feelings of sexual attraction, one manifestation of which I'll call "the Uncle Bill syndrome." When I was a college student, I spent several summers working at a popular mountain resort. During that time, because I was already interested in the priesthood, I got to know the parish priest, a man in his early fifties I will call Father Bill. Father Bill was extremely kind to me; he helped me find housing, permitted me occasional use of his car, often invited me (and a friend of mine with whom I was living at the time) to have dinner with him. He was really like a very generous uncle to a boy who was far from home and in need of a little care.

Although I didn't realize it the first summer of our relationship, this friendship was really based on homosexual attraction. As I look back now, I'm sure that Father Bill was as gay as I am, and that his generosity was really sublimated sexual attraction. While that doesn't diminish the force or quality of the friendship for me, it is an example of a particular, and rather common, expression of homosexuality among clergymen.

Father Bill's affection toward me was never a burden, nor did he ever "put the move" on me. There were a couple of times, however, when he hugged me just a bit too long or ardently or gazed at me a bit too intently; those times told me that we shared more than our religious vocation.

I never asked Father Bill if he was gay; it didn't even occur to me until well toward the end of our time together (he died shortly after I saw him last). Even if I had asked him, however, I'm quite sure he would have been shocked at the suggestion. I suspect he knew that he found men more attractive than women, but he had certainly not consciously articulated it. And even though an obviously gay couple would draw a comment such as "Look at those two!" from one or the other of us, that is as far as it went. Uncle Bill seemed to be able to channel his sexuality into productive, nonmanipulative, and mutual relationships with younger men he found attractive. In fact, that ability formed a strong bond between us, even though the basis for it remained unspoken. His sudden death was a great loss to me, and even today, nearly fifteen years later, I recall our times together with great warmth and gratitude, and consider my friendship with him one of the great blessings of my life.

I have discussed this relationship to suggest that sexual attraction can be a positive force, even among celibates. Though I certainly wouldn't have told many people that I thought my friendship with Father Bill was based on sexual attraction (even now it seems a bit crude to write it), it was nevertheless a factor in our relationship. Yet that attraction never led to any kind of genital activity, nor did Father Bill place any unreasonable or uncomfortable demands on me. In fact, his influence was one of the major factors in my decision to enter the seminary.

Some years later, when I was in the seminary, I encountered another kind of "Uncle Bill," whom I will call Father Smith. I'm quite sure Father Smith, who was over sixty when I met him, had never spoken about his gayness to anyone; yet, one night when I led him back to his room after he had drunk too much, he made it clear to me that he found young men attractive. Though we never referred to the incident later (it consisted only in a clumsy attempt at a kiss that I discouraged as gently as I could), Father Smith obviously had struggled with his sexuality for a long time, yet had not managed to sublimate it quite as successfully as Father Bill had.

In another variation on the "Uncle Bill" theme, a middle-aged priest repeatedly developed obsessive attractions to one or another of the seminarians. Although these relationships were never genital in nature, they were not pleasant ones for the seminarians involved. The relationships were demanding, jealous, exclusive, and cloying. At one point, the older priest's devotion was so persistent that supervisors had to intervene. Again, I'm sure the priest would have been highly offended had anyone accused him of homosexuality or "being gay," yet it seems quite clear to me that sexual attraction was exactly the energy behind his friendship for the young seminarian. Though not overtly genital, such relationships can be damaging on a number of fronts: they are frustrating to the older person, who sees his overtures and generosity constantly rejected; they create division among students, who resent the attention showered on one of their companions; and they can be extremely distressing to the young man, who doesn't wish to offend the older priest's kindness but is embarrassed by the gifts and attention and annoyed by the demands.

I want to emphasize at this point that while I believe there are a significant number of celibate relationships of the kind I have just described, that is, relationships "fueled" by sexual attraction, it is impossible to say where friendship begins and sexual attraction leaves off; as with any human friendships, the dynamics of those I have just described are complex and should not be judged from afar. When I say that sexual attraction "fueled" these relationships, I mean only that; such attraction may have sparked the relationship and energized it later on, but the attraction was not explicit and did not lead to sexual overtures.

A much more serious form of denial takes the form of hostility, either to oneself or to others, and very often toward other gay people. In its most introverted form, it is a more or less concerted self-hatred that might be manifest in rigorous self-denial, neglect of personal hygiene or grooming, overeating or drinking, severe and unrelenting penitential practices, hyperorthodoxy and inflexibility in religious beliefs, or compulsive attendance at liturgical functions. The personality behind this may be either passive and unfeeling or aggressive and judgmental, but in either case the person is trying to build up a wall of denial. I remember one priest who spent most of his years in the seminary reading his breviary (in Latin), saying his rosary, fasting, and maintaining a pasty and slovenly appearance. Shortly after his ordination he "discovered" his sexuality, left the community, and changed overnight into a muscle-bound, bleached-blond hustler. His was a classic case of this kind of introverted hostile denial.

This is not to suggest, of course, that everyone who is compulsive or hyperorthodox or a regular at morning prayer is a closet homosexual but it is to suggest that people who are running away from questions of sexuality often adopt these activities, and often make a most dramatic break with their previous life-style once they come out.

The other kind of hostile denial is more readily recognizable; it is directed outward rather than inward and entails attacks on everyone and everything that smacks of gayness. Most religious are familiar with the frequent "fag jokes" at dinner and in the recreation room; in my experience, they are often coverups by the people who are most insecure about their own sexuality and wish to locate homosexual feelings "out there." At its worst, this kind of denial takes the form of organized, public attacks on the character or way of life of gay people, and among teachers or preachers, may extend to lengthy, moralistic diatribes—usually as the teacher dispassionately "teaches" the immorality of homosexuality. Such attacks (which at the very least ignore the Church's distinction between person and act to which I referred earlier) not only are devastating to those present who might be gay, but also promote a mentality that quickly degenerates into "fag-beating" (and random violence against other minorities).

Although the occasional cases of homosexual child molesting by priests or ministers are always big news items, in fact such behavior is quite rare, and most often occurs among gay people who are not out and who do not discuss their inclinations with anyone. I know dozens of gay priests, but to my knowledge, only two have ever been involved in any way with children or adolescents; in both cases there had been no prior admission of homosexuality or any involvement with the gay "culture." I suspect that in many of these cases, we are really dealing with a kind of hostile denial of sexuality that leads to sexual abuse of children rather than reciprocal, peer relationships.

Qualified Acceptance

There are many people who have acknowledged their gayness, but only to a limited extent. While not manifesting the kind of denial I have described above, they have not yet fully integrated their gayness either. There are three distinguishable kinds of qualified acceptance in this group: admitting gayness only to oneself (intrapersonal acceptance); acknowledging it to others, but only on a very limited basis, for example, to one or two trusted friends or to a confessor (interpersonal acceptance); and, whether or not one acknowledges one's gayness to other people, indulging in promiscuous sexual behavior.

Intrapersonal acknowledgment. Most gay people, at some point, come to a conscious realization of their gayness; sometimes this realization occurs very early (perhaps even in adolescence), other times much later and only after a lengthy period of conscious or unconscious denial. Many gay people I know say that they "knew" they were gay as children; I remember clear feelings of attraction for boys as early as 8 or 9 years of age, and I cannot recall ever being attracted to girls. That awareness went unarticulated for many years, however, until one night when I was a freshman in college. I was having a discussion with a friend of mine who announced he was gay, and as soon as he said the word, I knew immediately that I was too. That signaled an "intrapersonal" acceptance—I had acknowledged the fact to myself—but it would be some time until I shared that with anyone else. Often this awareness develops when one falls in love with another man; it occurs at the point when one realizes that one's feelings for someone are more than friend-ship, and that the attraction is physical as well as social and emotional.

Many religious and priests, even though they are aware of their gayness, decide to keep their identity to themselves, usually out of fear of discovery. Still, this kind of gayness in religious life can be a positive force; it allows one to build stronger community ties on the basis of sexual attraction but moderates that attraction with restraint. The difference between this and the gay priest who has not admitted his proclivity is obvious: it seems to me that many times when feelings of attraction for someone of the same sex go unacknowledged, they degenerate into unhealthy compulsions or erupt sporadically in moments of weakness. In addition, unacknowledged sexual feelings are much more difficult to deal with psychologically. Certainly, openness about one's sexuality poses problems of its own, but lack of awareness (especially when homosexual feelings are masked under a heterosexual facade) creates an illusory identity upon which it is very difficult to build a solid spiritual or religious life.

If I approach celibacy, for example, convinced that I am only attracted to women, when my deepest inclinations are toward men, I have built a castle on sand. The self-deception that usually enters into such a construct is so profound that it can sometimes last a lifetime. If it doesn't, one's entire spiritual life can collapse. Even if it does last, going through life not knowing whether one is attracted to men or to women seems sterile at best. My suspicion is that in many cases, such lack of self-awareness is bought at a very high price, because in order to maintain it one must decide (even if unconsciously) to forgo many of the emotions that most people consider an essential part of life. The result is a kind of emotional neurasthenia that leads to burnout, frustration, and very little engagement with anyone of either sex, on any level.

Those who have admitted their sexuality, yet keep it to themselves, often do so to avoid the pain of "coming out," and to avoid having to reshuffle their entire lives in view of a new, overt sexual need. Often such a choice can be very prudent and can preserve a celibate vocation with a minimum of dishonesty and deceit. Someone who has made this choice is not likely to become preoccupied with sexuality, yet the attraction can, as I have pointed out, function in a positive way in community life and in personal relations. Nor is such a person likely to be part of a gay "subculture," which can be divisive in community life.

The problem with this mode of clerical gayness is that it can be very solitary; I have seen this kind of gayness only among people who are otherwise very strong and have a solid spiritual life. Most people require some kind of support if they are going to deal with sexuality openly, because the minute sexual desire is brought out in the open, it becomes a force to be reckoned with.

Interpersonal acknowledgment. A second kind of qualified accept-ance of one's gayness is admission of it to one or two close friends or to a spiritual director or confessor. Many see this as ideal; it allows a certain degree of openness and a chance to process difficulties with another person, but it avoids overiden-tification with the gay subculture. In my experience, however, someone at this level of acknowledgment rarely remains there; there are either romantic episodes ("falling in love") or occasional periods of some kind of sexual activity, and unless the confessor or director is very experienced in dealing with clerical gayness, it is unlikely that this one outlet for discussion will be adequate. The point is that sexuality is not merely a personal matter but a social one, and it usually needs to be integrated into a broader context than a one-on-one relation-ship. To invoke another analogy, it seems likely that a child who only discussed sex with one other person would probably end up emotionally or psychologically stunted; the interaction with other people, in a social setting, is vital to healthy development.

Promiscuity. Many celibates who have only a partial or private understanding of their sexual identity cope with it secretly in numerous and anonymous sexual liaisons. Far from the control characteristic of the last group we discussed, the members of this group of gay celibates fear discovery too much to disclose their sexuality to anyone, yet regularly seek sex in public restrooms, secluded parks, gay baths, or elsewhere. This is certainly the least healthy type of "qualified acceptance," for it not only requires a double life, which creates great emotional strain, but exposes the priest to the very real dangers of arrest, entrapment, blackmail, venereal disease, and, if the priest's worst fears are realized, discovery by a parishioner or student who happens to be in search of the same kind of sexual activity.

At its worst, this type of "acceptance" is really no acceptance at all, for it is coupled with hostility toward gay people and an aggressively "straight' public identity. It has always been a mystery to me how people who spend several nights a week in search of anonymous gay sex in very dangerous places can come home and make suggestive comments about the physical endowments of the girl who works in the parish office, yet it happens. And while the risks of entrapment and blackmail don't seem to scare them, they are terrified by the thought of going into a gay bar for a drink. Anonymity allows them to console themselves with the thought that they are "not really gay" but just out for a good time or for sexual release. Apparently for many of these people, facing the vice squad is less of a threat than facing other gay people—and their own gay identity.

I might add that although promiscuous sexual behavior is sometimes found in people who have only partly acknowledged their sexuality, it is also prevalent among those who have, apparently, fully accepted their gayness. I say apparently because it seems to me that promiscuity almost always signals some lack of integration of one's sexuality. Even if one has socially admitted one's gayness, promiscuous behavior is often a manifestation of deep dissatisfaction, lack of acceptance, or low self-image. James B. Nelson, in his book *Embodiment*, says that this kind of impersonal sex is really "impersonal lunges, by an ego already torn apart under the pressure of various conflicts, at reestablishing some emotional links with the world . . . [they are] efforts of the shattered self to salvage something—almost anything—of natural emotional relationships."[1]

Full Acceptance

The final group with which we will be concerned consists of those priests who have socially acknowledged their sexuality, who have gay friends, who are or have been sexually active, and who are more or less aware of the gay subculture. These priests frequently disclose their orientation to one or more straight friends, as well, although typically this occurs some time after coming out.

We might distinguish several subgroups here, too, but this time they are based upon whether the priest came out before he entered the seminary, while he was in the seminary, or after ordination. In all three of these categories (and among gay people in general) I have noted a general "coming out" pattern. Although it is only a paradigm, I would say that nearly all gay people who "come out" go through the following stages of progressively more explicit gay identity.

Initial acknowledgment. This sometimes begins with an acknowledgment of "bisexuality," which is slightly more acceptable in our society than homosexuality. As I have already noted, however, true bisexuality is very rare, and in some cases an admission of it is merely transitional; it is short-lived and usually doesn't even involve any sexual experience with the opposite sex, although it often does include and may have been occasioned by, a sexual encounter with someone of the same sex.

This initial acknowledgment, which is crucial (the first question asked of someone who admits being gay is How do you know?), is parallel to the "intrapersonal" acknowledgment I mentioned earlier and is extremely complex. Virtually every gay man I have known says he knew "very early" (usually by the age of 10, sometimes even earlier), but exactly how this awareness emerges, or why, is a mystery. I have long felt that sexual identity is determined very early in childhood and may even be the result of genetic factors. In my own case, which I described earlier, I had been aware of my attraction to men, and even experienced sexual arousal as a young high school student; it was not until college, however, that I was able to name the experience. Many other gays say that although they knew they were attracted to men, they thought they were the only people in the world who were and only acknowledged it as a psychological state after reading about it in a magazine or book. Today, of course, gayness is much more widely discussed, and presumably that will make acknowledgment easier. I am confident that increased societal awareness of homosexuality will not, however, lead to "accidental" gayness among adolescents. Sexual identity is not a matter of choice.

However or whenever it happens, there is at some point a shift to a more or less explicit awareness of oneself as gay; there may be a little more sexual activity (usually clandestine and discussed only in confessional, if at all) and perhaps a first tentative visit to a gay bar or contact with other gay people in a social setting.

Retreat. In many cases the person becomes frightened or repulsed by the whole experience, because initial encounters with something you've been hiding for any number of years can be rather intimidating, and this leads to what I'd call a "retreat to the closet," a fervent wish that it weren't so and a desperate unhappiness and confusion, often precipitated by social or familial hostility to homosexuality. There's usually a strong determination to "change," and at this point many gay people seek counseling or some other kind of professional help, while steadfastly avoiding gay people and the gay scene. If the person has been involved with someone sexually, that person is usually the particular focus of the rejection and may be bewildered and shocked by the sudden turn of events.

This stage may last as long as a year or more, and the sequence of "acknowledgment-retreat" may be repeated several times. While I think most gay people experience ambivalent feelings about coming out, the "in and out" syndrome I have just described is usually more prolonged and the attitude changes more marked in people with strong religious backgrounds. This is due, I suppose, to residual religious guilt about homosexuality.. Those with ethnic religious backgrounds often find the transition even more difficult, and generally men find it more difficult than women.

Emergence. Final emergence from these radical attitude changes is usually accompanied by some kind of regular participation in gay culture (usually gay friends and gay bars) and regular sexual activity, although the frequency and number of sexual partners varies greatly.

After a period of sexual experimentation, there are usually one or more relatively long-term sexual relationships (lovers) and a number of close gay friendships, which are almost always nonsexual and which serve as the gay person's primary support group. These friendship groups tend to be very close-knit and protective; they provide continuity between lovers (who, unfortunately, come and go) as well as many of the emotional supports that one usually finds in a family, because gay people often don't reveal their gayness to their families and, even if they do, don't always find understanding.

Stability. The final stage of coming out (which may not occur until years after the initial revelation) is the development of a stable behavior pattern. By stable I don't necessarily mean "married"; the stability that evolves at this point may or may not be healthy. It could entail a committed relationship with one person, celibacy lived in or outside a religious community or the priesthood, or a relatively promiscuous sex life. At this stage, however, there is usually a significant degree of identity with gay culture and gay friends and comfort with being gay. What characterizes this stage is the emergence of a pattern of behavior, whatever particular form it may take. If one is inclined to relatively short-term or even promiscuous relationships, that will probably continue; if one finds most satisfaction in a relatively celibate existence with numerous nonsexual friendships, that is likely to remain the case; and if one has or has had a lover, one will probably continue to have a lover, or find life difficult without one.

These stages are not unique to gay people; I expect one could construct a similar chart for any adolescent and indicate some point at which a "pattern " of affective behavior was established, whether it be marriage, divorce and remarriage, promiscuity, or celibacy. The difference is that the whole process usually takes place much later among gay people and involves considerably more stress, both because age makes such transitions more difficult and because one is moving into an identity that does not enjoy wide social acceptance.

I must emphasize at this point that what I have described above is not "choosing to be gay"; it is not a question of one day deciding that one will be straight or gay. Just as heterosexuals don't "choose" to be that way, so gay people don't either. At most, they are able to choose to what extent they will acknowledge their gayness—to themselves, to friends, to business associates—and how they will live it out. I am convinced that gay identity, whatever its origins, is established very early (probably before 5 years of age). In the vast majority of cases, there is no changing it beyond that point. I know many gay people who have sought psychiatric or psychological counseling; I know none who have "changed." The only choice is about acknowledgment and disclosure.

The Consequences of Awareness

Having briefly sketched what I perceive as a coming out pattern, I will now apply that pattern to the three situations I described earlier, starting with priests who come out after ordination—in my estimation, the most difficult of the three.

Priests Who Come Out After Ordination

Social disapproval of homosexuality always makes coming out difficult, and it is even more difficult for someone who is planning to be celibate, or who has just vowed himself to celibacy, as has the newly ordained priest, because coming out, or developing a *social* sexual identity, usually involves some kind of sexual activity. Taking a vow of celibacy and suddenly discovering that one has done so under false pretenses can be very distressing. All the plans and hopes constructed during seminary years seem jeopardized as one realizes that celibacy doesn't have to do with women but with men. It's like starting all over again.

Such a realization is bad enough in itself, but it usually hits the priest at a particularly vulnerable time in his life. Not only is he in the midst of adjusting to the exercise of new authority and new responsibility and to the general shift from seminary life to rectory life, but he is also without the support of the friends, confidants, and spiritual directors who were part of his seminary years. The loneliness that often plagues the newly ordained priest in his first years after ordination is aggravated by this new awareness of his sexuality. Not only does he yearn for the companionship that was so readily available in the dormitory atmosphere of the seminary, but also he now finds he has to cope with entirely new feelings of sexual attraction to men. Nor does he feel free to discuss his feelings with either the pastor or parishioners.

The dangers in this state of affairs should be obvious. Just at the most vulnerable moment of his priestly life, the young priest is confronted with powerful feelings of sexual attraction and few means to deal with them. At the very least, the priest's ministry will be disrupted. Though he may be versatile enough to maintain his duties without apparent difficulty, the psychic energy expended on resolving his dilemma will take its toll. In the most extreme cases, guilt and anxiety about the incompatibility of his feelings with his vows will lead to a breakdown or to departure from the ordained ministry. I know of one priest who left the ministry only months after he was ordained when he finally decided, on his own, that his homosexuality was simply incompatible with priesthood. Though such a drastic measure could have been avoided if he had consulted with someone else, it illustrates how profound a crisis realizing his gay identity can be for a conscientious young priest, especially when he is isolated from peers and superiors and thinks he is the only gay priest in the world.

More commonly, however, priests who come out after ordination go through some kind of socialization into the gay subculture—bars, friendships, or sexual activity. Though often less traumatic than the scenario I described above, this process can still be draining and debilitating as the priest tries to decide how to incorporate this new factor into his ministerial life. The dilemma is usually resolved in one of three ways: anonymous sexual activity, a "double life," or departure from celibate ministry.

Anonymity. Similar to the anonymous sexual activity I described above, anonymity as an attempt to cope with homosexuality after ordination is an incomplete, unhealthy approach that revolves around clandestine, anonymous sexual encounters calculated to cause the least disruption to ministry. To the casual observer, there would be no change at all. The priest choosing this approach would simply take care of his sexual needs in the most impersonal way possible, avoiding entangling gay relationships that would lead to complications. This approach, as I have already suggested, is usually destructive and unhealthy, and symptomatic of other problems.

The double life. Unfortunately, the double life is fairly common; the priest either is unwilling to end his ministry or afraid to because of his vows or family pressure, yet is also unwilling (or unable) to live the celibacy he chose before he was aware of his gayness. In this case, he chooses a compromise: remain ostensibly celibate, but have an intimate lover, a gay friend, or at least a gay social life "on the side." A "lover" can refer to anyone from a close friend with whom one does not live but with whom one has occasional physical intimacy, to someone approaching a spouse, who lives in the same house and with whom one has a regular sexual life. Needless to say, having a lover while continuing to live a celibate, rectory way of life can be extremely taxing, and unfair to the lover, who can never expect a full commitment from the priest. Maintaining a clandestine gay life on the side is less so, but carries with it the fear of discovery and a very real potential for scandal.

Many others, like myself, were "out" before entering religious life, yet still chose to do so. They, too, often live a double life, but one more consciously chosen, usually as a response to the loneliness and solitude that is an inherent part of celibate life. Since ordination, I have tried at various times to establish more or less intimate relationships with quasi-lovers. I have found it impossible and have pretty much abandoned that option as unfeasible. Aside from the theoretical conflict between my vows as a religious and an ongoing sexual relationship, I found the logistics and the emotional demands too heavy. In reality, my community is my main priority, and I could not be faithful to community demands and to a lover (or even an intense gay friendship) at the same time.

However, I sympathize with other priests, who came out after ordination but do not have communities or peers to support them, who have chosen to commit themselves to a more or less stable relationship. It is very difficult to remain perfectly celibate and yet sensitive, emotionally responsive, and happy. It seems that far too often one either remains perfectly celibate or emotionally alive; balancing the two is very difficult and achievement of balance is truly a sign of sanctity. Many others have found their ministry aided and their road to sanctity illuminated by intimate, relatively stable relationships.

I hesitate to condemn priests if they have adopted that lifestyle after due consideration, balanced the demands of their ministry with those of the relationship, and established a mutual, trusting relationship with another person. This last qualification is important, because the priest's gay friend can easily become a therapeutic instrument for the priest, who, unable to fully commit himself because of his life-style and ministerial commitments, "uses" the friend for his own emotional satisfaction. However, while I can tolerate such arrangements as concessions to an imperfect world, they should not be entered into easily or lightly, and this for a number of reasons.

First of all, there is what we call the grace of the sacrament. Such traditional language may seem strangely out of place in an essay such as this, but there is still the reality behind the term that has an important place in this discussion. Grace is God's experienced presence, and the grace of vocational sacraments such as marriage or ordination is God's presence toward the fulfillment of the call one incurs in the reception of those sacraments. Just as the grace of marriage is what enables couples to overcome difficulties, persevere in fidelity, and grow in love, so the grace of ordination helps the priest not only to discharge his ministerial duties but also to live a life worthy of one who serves as a leader in the Christian community.

I do not mean to imply that being gay is unworthy of the Christian community—far from it. But I do mean to say that in fact the priest has committed himself publicly to celibacy, and that, as a rule, people will expect that from him. Many today argue that celibacy is a charism and should never have been juridically imposed as a condition for ordination; that is probably true. However, once having committed himself to celibacy, the priest should do all he can to try to preserve that commitment, and recourse to prayer and the sacrament of reconciliation should be his first steps.

The second reason establishing a lover relationship should be done only as a last resort is stress. Stress is a problem for all priests, who, like many professionals, have irregular and demanding schedules that make it difficult to carve out time to spend with families and spouses. Emotional obligations to a lover aggravate that problem and can lead to a "9 to 5" mentality on the part of the priest, who finds he wants more and more time with his friend and has less and less time for his parishioners.

The problem can be even worse for priests who live in communities, since community life usually affords less personal freedom and imposes real obligations of time and effort apart from ministry. Religious priests who try to develop close, demanding relationships outside of community are usually headed for a nervous breakdown, a confrontation with their community, or a great deal of hostility from their brothers, who may not know that there is "another man" but still sense the drain of energy and the fact that the priest's life is focused not in the community but elsewhere.

The final, and perhaps most serious, problem with priests who have lovers is the lover himself. As should be clear by now, it is the rare priest who will be versatile and energetic enough to sustain a lover relationship and be faithful to his ministerial duties. But even if he manages to do that with success, it will require the tolerant cooperation of a lover who is willing to settle for half a relationship. In all likelihood, the two will not be able to live together; they will probably spend a lot of free time together, but the commitment will always be limited by the demands of the priest's ministry (and community life, if he is a religious priest). Even if the lover is willing to accept these terms, it seems to me that they impose unacceptable restrictions on the relationship.

Two people planning to get married, for example, could never do so under such circumstances; the commitment required for marriage would either have to be total—"in sickness and in health," and so on—or not at all. Whether such a limited commitment as characterizes these clerical relationships is either charitable or just is highly questionable. I said I sympathize with priests who choose this route as a compromise, rather than leaving the priesthood altogether, but I have seen their lovers hurt and betrayed because of the limitations that priesthood places on such relationships, and I think we must ask seriously whether these relationships can ever be fair to the priest's lover.

A final variation of this approach is a priest and another priest becoming "lovers." I believe this type of relationship has the best chance of survival, because the two priests share the same values, have similar ministerial commitments, and can support each other's spiritual lives; their relationship is less likely to be detected than that of a priest and an unattached man who spend a great deal of time together. Although they are only lovers in an analogical sense because they often don't live together (and even if they do must maintain the appearance of being just "friends"), I believe that their relationship can be valuable; in fact, there is some evidence that formal ratification of such "dedicated friendships" among priests existed in medieval religious communities, and that they were seen as broadly sacramental.[2]

Although arguably at odds with current understandings of celibacy, these relationships seem to be able to provide support, encouragement, and energy for celibate ministers; in my experience, priests involved in such committed relationships (which tend to become progressively less genital) seem to be happier and more productive in their work than are their uncommitted counterparts. The relationships seem to provide a modicum of security, stability, and warmth in a life that is often defined by its transience and lack of attachment.

Positive as these relationships can be, however, they are not without difficulties; they can lead to stress and feelings of guilt; in community, they can give rise to jealousy and resentment; and if one of the partners is transferred or leaves the community, the resulting disruption can be very painful and even precipitate a vocational crisis, because the relationship often becomes important enough to displace ministry as the primary focus of one's life. Despite this, however, and even though "particular friendships" were one of the great horrors of the old seminary system, I think these committed relationships between two priests, even if overtly genital, can be a tolerable solution to the problems of loneliness, isolation, and frustration that often plague celibate priests.

Resignation from the priesthood. The final group we must consider are those priests who come out after ordination and feel compelled to leave the priesthood or their religious communities. Sometimes this happens as a result of overwhelming feelings of guilt, as the priest realizes he is gay and sees this as absolutely incompatible with his consecrated state of life. In this case, he may flee suddenly, with no real explanation to anyone.

Far more often, however, the priest comes out, begins the process of socialization into the gay scene, and realizes that his need for intimacy is much stronger than his desire for priesthood; in fact, he may even realize in retrospect that his decision to enter the seminary was only an attempt to build a respectable life in view of a subconscious awareness of his homosexuality. I suspect this was often the case in the past if a young man realized early on that he was not likely to get married; before the days of open discussion of homosexuality and the gay life-style, he could easily have interpreted this to mean that he "had a vocation" and entered the seminary. Only later, as he became aware that gay people had gained some measure of respectability in society would he be able to face the fact of his own gayness.

Often, concurrent realization of one's gayness and of the possibility of a respectable life as a gay person outside the priesthood combine to create an overwhelming urgency. Although the awareness that would lead to departure may have been growing for some time, it reaches a crisis rapidly, which makes the priest feel he can't put up with celibacy or ministerial demands one moment longer. In these cases, departure from ministry is often precipitous and sometimes even rash. In one case I recall, the priest had only been ordained six weeks when he "knew" he had to leave. Once that decision was reached, there was no negotiation; it was over. Even though some opportunity had been available for discussion of sexuality in his seminary years, family expectations, the formation "structure," and his own need to see it through to ordination prevented him from coming to terms with his identity and his needs earlier.

Many bishops and religious superiors are astonished at the frequency with which these early departures are occurring today. Some groups report attrition rates approaching 50 percent in the first five years; not only is this a drain on morale, but on finances as well, because the cost of seminary education is approaching $15,000 per year. As should be apparent by now, the factors contributing to these departures are complex, and no single step will likely provide a remedy. However, I will make a couple of suggestions.

First of all, it should be clear that seminaries do not "make" people gay. While they may create an atmosphere in which one can more easily come to terms with homosexual feelings (including the absence of pressure to date and marry), the seminary system is not totally at fault, though it is possible that a more open system of education would attract candidates of more varied emotional makeup.

What seminaries (and ministry) do, however, is encourage development of gifts that are "feminine" in the Jungian sense— creativity, sensitivity, receptivity, intuitiveness—qualities that are not elicited in men in the society at large. As these inclinations (which are latently present in everyone) are summoned to the surface and cultivated for use in ministry, sexual attraction may arise among gay candidates, too. Always there, these "feminine" attributes now become explicit, and with them, any latent homosexual attraction. In heterosexual candidates, these same qualities are cultivated, but no sexual attraction emerges.

One big problem is discontinuity between the seminary and the first assignment. This is especially true where seminary formation follows a rigorous, monastic pattern that allows little freedom. Once ordained, the seminarian is not equipped to handle all the freedom of a first assignment, and intimacy needs may explode, catching him unawares and leading to one of the unhappy solutions I have outlined.

At least some seminary administrations have responded to the alarming number of early departures from the priesthood by tightening the reins on seminaries—restricting seminarians' associations with one another, issuing ultimatums about gay activity, bar-going, and "camping," and rigidly avoiding discussion of the matter, privately or publicly. Far from alleviating the problem, this approach seems to have set the stage for the precipitous departures, scandals, or confrontations that have been occurring with undue frequency. The tighter the control on behavior and integration of sexual identity during seminary years, the more likely the young priest is to deal with it inappropriately when he finally does come out, often in the relative freedom of the parish or teaching situation of his first assignment.

There is no way to prevent gay candidates from applying for admission to the seminary or religious life, and probably no way to detect them in advance. As I have pointed out, in many cases, the candidates themselves are not aware of their gayness. And even if it were possible to detect gay candidates in order to screen them out, I hope this essay successfully argues that it would hardly be desirable to do so. However, seminary officials and religious superiors can reduce untimely departures to a minimum by encouraging open and frank discussion of sexuality, sexual identity, and sexual needs prior to ordination. Such discussion may reveal some candidates who are gay, and who realize they need more time before they make their decision, or who simply decide they cannot pursue ordination. But at the very least every candidate, by the time he is ordained, should know what his sexual orientation is (even if he has revealed it to no one else) and be quite certain that he can fulfill the demands of ministry and celibacy given that orientation. Although such openness carries with it the "risk" that seminarians will discover they are gay, making that discovery while in formation before permanent commitments are made seems vastly preferable to making the discovery alone, in the first vulnerable months of priesthood.

Inevitably, however, there will be priests whose sexuality emerges only after ordination. When that happens, the reaction of superiors is often anger, fear, or panic. In one case with which I am familiar, a young priest came out two years after ordination. When the bishop found out he had been frequenting bars, he transferred him to another parish, far from the city, but never discussed the fact of his gayness with him. A second incident occasioned a discussion of sexuality in very general terms, and another transfer. The bishop, unable to address the issue directly, avoided it, and hoped it would just "go away." Such an approach is like hiding a bottle from an alcoholic (though the analogy here is not a very good one): remove the source of temptation, and the attraction will cease. Most will agree that this is not a very effective way to treat chemical dependency, nor is it an effective way to deal with a gay priest.

First of all, refusal to discuss sexuality and sexual needs combined with repeated transfers place the priest in a position of dependency and discourage accountability. "If the bishop is going to transfer me every time I mess up," the priest may reason, "then why should I make any effort to change?" Since he's being treated like a child, he's likely to continue to act like one—both out of frustration at being given no share in his own future and out of anger at a superior who won't acknowledge his worth as a gay person. Although affirmation from a bishop or superior isn't going to bring the priest to immediate integration of his gay sexuality, it is hard to overestimate the difference that simple acceptance can make for the priest. Not only is he being treated as an adult who has just encountered a personality factor that may make his priestly life more complicated, but he is also allowed the space and dignity to make sensible decisions that respect his commitments. Anger, thinly veiled disgust, and avoidance on the part of the superior can easily push a priest to subconscious retaliation in promiscuity, indiscretion, or departure from the priesthood.

The superior's own gayness can aggravate the problem, especially if he is unaware of it. It is no secret that some of the greatest hostility and homophobia is found in people who are themselves gay; if a superior experiences strong emotional reactions to a subordinate's homosexuality, he should carefully examine his own life for similar feelings; fear of his own homosexuality can be a real impediment to justice in dealing with a gay candidate or priest in his care. If all else fails, he should refer the case to a colleague who can handle it with more equanimity.

If, despite all attempts at integration, the young priest still feels compelled to leave the ministry, he should be encouraged to do so. Whenever possible, he should take a leave of absence before making a final decision, and lines of communication should be kept open so that he will feel free to return at some point in the future. Often a year or two away from ministry will give him the chance to place his gayness in perspective, realize that ministry (and community life) are still important values for him, and discover that he's willing to subordinate his new sexual needs to them.

If he does leave the active ministry, however, and more or less adopt a "gay life-style," he should be aware of the possibility of scandal. In one case I remember, a friend left the priesthood shortly after ordination. While I was at dinner with a parishioner some weeks later, he unexpectedly asked about the former priest, "I heard Father John is queer. Is that true?" Even when priests leave the ministry, they retain an obligation to protect the reputation of those who remain. There will be inevitable misunderstandings, but gay priests on leaves of absence should take some care to avoid scandal, especially when they remain in the city in which they served as priests.

Coming Out in the Seminary

Coming out in an environment in which one should be working on growth in celibacy and the spiritual life is far from ideal. It is a major distraction, often disrupts study and spiritual life, and because coming out usually entails sexual activity, or at least adoption of a sexual identity, runs counter to much of seminary formation, which is geared to celibacy; still, it is preferable to coming out after ordination.

Though sexual identity should not be a public matter, responsible seminary formation will encourage discussion of it. As I have already suggested, frankness and honesty are probably the most important tools in seminary training today, and unless we see body and soul as completely separate, one's body and one's sexual needs must be integrated into "spiritual" formation. Discussion of sexuality will not cause a mass exodus from the closet, but it may help avoid trauma and confusion after ordination.

The topic of sexuality almost always emerges at some point in spiritual direction or counseling; when it does, it should be gently explored, and when possible, the spiritual director (respecting confidentiality, of course) should encourage the directee to discuss his orientation, or question about his orientation, in a wider forum—perhaps sessions organized on a regular basis for discussion of matters pertinent to formation. If no student is willing to discuss his own questions, the director should broach the subject of intimacy needs, with specific reference to homosexuality, in a gentle and nonjudgmental way, perhaps by asking "What if?" kinds of questions. An article or book on the topic might be a helpful preparation. Seminarians who are experiencing homosexual feelings are not likely to talk about it at the first session, or perhaps ever. But at least they must know that they can talk about it should the need arise.

Discussion of the topic of homosexuality can be intensely uncomfortable for everyone. A straight director may not feel competent to discuss it (though the issues of intimacy and attraction are the same for straights as for gays), and a marginally gay priest may find it too threatening. In such cases, the director should not hesitate to enlist the help of a gay priest who feels more comfortable discussing it. He need not reveal the fact that he is gay (though to do so would be helpful, since there are so few role models for gay priests), but his relative familiarity with the subject should enable him to pose and field questions more easily.

A big concern in seminaries today is gay bars, or more specifically, seminarians who go to gay bars. In a very real sense, gay bars are no different from other bars; more often than not, they are places for socializing and are not necessarily geared to picking up sexual partners. They play a more prominent role in gay life than in straight life, however, because they provide a refuge from the constant vigilance that gay people must maintain if their friends, co-workers, and clients don't know they are gay. Gay bars have always been for me a place where I can be exactly who I am without fear of recrimination, ridicule, or misunderstanding. Gay bars are not simply "meat racks" whose customers seek only sexual gratification, but ghettos where there is security in numbers and in shared identity.

If one understands that, then it is easier to understand the great attraction that bars hold for many people. Although most gay people eventually develop a social circle and spend more time at home parties and in other non-bar situations, that is usually not an option for the very young (who are not yet established, and may even live at home) or for those who live in institutional settings, like seminarians. For them, the bars can be an important gathering place and source of affirmation.

Clearly, however, celibates who go to gay bars give mixed signals. Even if they are there with a group and have no intention of "picking someone up," their presence can still be misconstrued and can foster a noncelibate approach to priesthood. What should a bishop or religious superior do if one of his students is frequenting the bars?

First of all, he should not issue an ultimatum. This usually precludes discussion and creates a suspension of trust, and probably will go unobeyed. He should, as I have repeatedly emphasized, encourage discussion of the risks, of the mixed signals, of the needs that underlie bar-going. Such a discussion can help foster responsibility and contribute to a real discernment process as the student moves toward ordination. In addition, this discussion should take place on the lowest level of authority possible. Sexuality issues are often "escalated," handled at higher levels than need be, which heightens anxiety and increases the chance of scandal, resentment, and noncommunication. If the matter comes to the attention of the spiritual director, it should be handled there and not referred to the rector or bishop unless absolutely necessary; if the rector or local superior finds out about it, it should be discussed there and not referred to the provincial or bishop. In one case, two seminarians who were caught sleeping together were referred further and further up until the case eventually reached Rome. Not only does such escalation make a mountain out of a molehill, it also generates paperwork and consumes energy that could much more fruitfully be expended elsewhere.

The superior should also realize that bar-going is often symptomatic of repression at home; if the gay student feels unwanted, suspect, and unworthy, the ghetto mentality takes over, and the bars become a real attraction. On the other hand, if gay students are accepted, allowed to associate (respecting the sensibilities of straight students, of course), and encouraged to talk about how they can be good priests, much of the reason for going to a bar disappears.

Although I have already indicated that gay friendships among priests can be a helpful support in ministry, such friendships in the seminary are often problematic, both because of the community situation and because of the relative immaturity of the seminarians. Often gay relationships take on the appearance of high school dating: they are passing, superficial, and hurtful and can be a great source of bitterness and jealousy.

When these relationships do occur (and they may be genital or not—the important thing is the level of intensity), they should be addressed coolly, without hysteria or recrimination, and as a normal part of the seminarian's spiritual growth.

Whenever possible, they should not be left as mere confessional matter; that is dealing with only half the issue. Of course, such a relationship, when revealed in confession, cannot be brought beyond that point without the consent of the penitent. However, the confessor should make every attempt to encourage the penitent to meet with him and the other half of the relationship—not with a view to "breaking it up" but to process it and look at it realistically in light of their celibate lives. Again, the confessor should not attempt this if he is uncomfortable with the topic or with intimacy between men.

Coming Out Before the Seminary

Acceptance of gay candidates for priesthood or religious life is an important topic, but I could hardly improve upon the excellent discussion of the matter by Fr. Basil Pennington.[3] I will therefore make only a few observations.

It is unrealistic to expect radical change in gay candidates who are accepted for the seminary or religious life. While even candidates who have had lovers or who have been sexually active prior to admission to religious life or the seminary can find the transition relatively easy and make excellent priests, the difficulty of the change should not be underestimated. As I have pointed out, patterns established by the time of application are likely to remain stable, and dramatic conversions or "shedding" of a gay identity are unlikely. Absolute certainty about one's ability to live celibately, to abandon the bar scene, and so on, should be viewed with circumspection (as indeed such dogmatism should be in any candidate).

This is not to say, however, that gay candidates are unacceptable or that they should be rejected out of hand. All things considered, they make excellent prospects because of the high degree of satisfaction they can derive from male companionship and because of other characteristics that I will discuss shortly. Overall, I doubt that their adjustment to celibacy is any more difficult or unlikely than is the adjustment of the typical heterosexual candidate.

I am amazed at how few diocese and religious groups will accept candidates who admit to being gay; many are forced into lying about their sexual identity in order to be considered for admission. It should be clear that admissions procedures or vocation directors who provoke that kind of response are not only losing valuable candidates but also starting the whole formation process off on very shaky ground.

Once again, a policy of considering gay people for admission need not be public; nor should sexual orientation be the exclusive focus of the admissions process—it is one factor to consider among others. The admissions process should focus, first, on the candidate's desire and suitability for ministry; that is, whether he can do the kind of work priests in this situation do and whether he wants to do it.

Second, it should focus on the candidate's desire and ability to live celibately, which includes a discussion of previous sexual experience and identity. The vocations director should not try to make absolutely certain judgments here; likelihood is good enough, and in doubtful cases, the candidate should be given the benefit of the doubt, since one of the purposes of the formation program is discernment and testing of a vocation. Even previous sexual experience or a "lover" should not disqualify a gay candidate. Motivation can be a powerful factor and can, in many cases, enable a previously "married" candidate to assume a celibate or community existence with satisfaction and happiness.

Gay Sexuality and the Religious Life

In this section, I would like to deal with what I have found to be important factors in the high correlation between gayness and service professions, especially the celibate ministry. I have already mentioned the need for respectability or to "atone" for one's homosexuality that (at least in the past) led many gay people to seek the priesthood as "the only way out." However, there are other, more profound reasons, which are eloquently summarized by Carl Jung in a well-known passage:

If we take the concept of homosexuality out of its narrow psycho-pathological setting and give it a wider connotation, we can see that it has positive aspects as well. . . . [It] gives him a great capacity for friendship, which often creates astonishing tenderness between men, and may even rescue friendship between the sexes from its limbo of the impossible. He may have good taste and an aesthetic sense which are fostered by the presence of a feminine streak. Then he may be supremely gifted as a teacher because of his almost feminine insight and tact. He is likely to have a feeling for history, and to be conservative in the best sense and cherish the values of the past. Often he is endowed with a wealth of religious feelings which help him to bring the *ecclesia spiritualis* into reality, and a spiritual receptivity which makes him responsive to revelation.[4]

Jung articulates reasons for something that many of us know: that gay people are found in greater numbers in certain professions, probably because of the "ascendancy of the feminine" and corresponding manifestation of characteristics that we do not usually associate with maleness. This is not to associate male homosexuality with femininity; Jung is speaking here of traits that are stereotypically or archetypally associated with men (aggressiveness, domination, etc.) and with women (passivity, sensitivity) but found in varying degrees in every-one. In my opinion, good priests, even when excessively macho in appearance and demeanor, must possess a healthy feminine dimension. Indeed, most men need to develop this Jungian "feminine" side.

We have all heard jokes about gay florists and hairdressers but there is something here. I don't want to imply that gay people are better suited for ministry than straight people, but I believe that in general there are a number of qualities that typically characterize gay people that both make ministry attractive to them and make them suitable for it. Although doubtless better words could be found, I will refer to these characteristics as sensitivity, adaptability, spirituality, and creativity.

Sensitivity. When I was a child, one of our parish priests (as I look back on it) was probably gay; at least he was slightly effeminate in mannerism, very soft-spoken, and very kind. Once, trying to describe him to a neighbor, my mother said, "You know, the sensitive one." The qualities she was referring to were those that have typically come to be identified with gay men, qualities like soft-spokenness, gentleness, articulateness, and passivity, qualities that (sometimes unfortunately) are not often associated with or encouraged in "normal" men.

I don't know where this "sensitivity" originates in gay men; to be sure, it is not absent in straight men, just less apparent. Perhaps it arises from the pain that comes from realizing that one is different, that one is a "sissy," that one can't "do what the other boys do." My own mother had the most annoying habit of telling me I was "sissified," which may have been true but that certainly caused me a lot of unhappiness. That, no doubt, contributed to whatever sensitivity I now possess.

That creeping awareness of being different also engendered an acute sensitivity to others' reactions—gay people grow up realizing that they have to constantly be aware of hostility or rejection from others and adjust their behavior accordingly. They also have to learn to spot subtle cues from other gay people in mixed social situations; they do this, not in search of a partner, but in search of a kindred spirit, much as one American in a crowd of foreigners seeks out another.

The usefulness of this sensitivity—both to suffering and to other's reactions—as a ministerial tool should be obvious, since much of ministry involves sensing suffering or unspoken cries for help and responding to them. Gay people are not the only ones whose sensitivity has been honed by suffering or humiliation or who are particularly adept at understanding unspoken language, but they often excel at it, and that talent can serve them well in ministry.

Adaptability. Like sensitivity, adaptability can be a "survival instinct," since it arises from living as a gay person in a world that does not accept homosexuality. At its worst, this "adaptability" is the kind of double life I described earlier. At its best, however, it develops into an ability to relate to a broad range of people and to draw on a broad variety of personality characteristics to fit the situation. Changing to fit the occasion may seem dishonest, but in fact we all have to do it, more or less. The lawyer or post office worker certainly relates differently to clients than to family—and to his wife differently than to his mother or his children. Gay people have the added dimension of homosexuality to incorporate, and because they live, work, and associate with people who are not gay, they must be able to adapt their behavior to both gay and nongay situations. That requires both quick judgment and better than average flexibility.

As I noted, everyone has to adjust to different kinds of people and different expectations. I think gay people do it on a grander scale, however. For instance, the average straight person is not comfortable (at least initially) with people he or she knows are gay; nor are close, emotional friendships common between two men (or even between a man and a woman who are not sexually involved, unfortunately). Gay men, on the other hand, often have the ability to relate well on all three levels: with straight people, with men, and with women. The gay ghetto is too small to permit anyone to have exclusively gay relationships, so the affective spectrum must be broadened. I suppose one could describe this as a kind of androgyny, since the gay man (and woman) must draw on both male and female personality factors in order to assemble an adequate social circle.

These skills are useful, because ministry is often

"superficial"—the minister has to establish a relatively intimate relationship quickly in order to deal with the problem at hand. Gay people—who have had to learn to relate to a wide variety of people on numerous levels of intimacy—may be able to do this more easily than straight people, whose relationships are more conventional. Growing up gay and learning to fit in with lots of people unlike yourself is probably a good preparation for ministry.

Spirituality. Jung describes gay men as having "a wealth of religious feelings which help him bring the *ecclesia spiritualis* into reality . . . and a spiritual receptivity which makes him responsive to revelation." Though I don't know the reason for it, I have noted that gay men are usually deeply spiritual—even if they are not explicitly religious. Perhaps it is merely prominence of the archetypal feminine receptivity, as Jung implies; perhaps there is a bit of the desperation that often leads the poor to be deeply religious, because they have nothing "in this world." But whatever it is, it never ceases to amaze me how often religion—or at least the transcendent— comes up in gay conversation.

Even gays who are overtly hostile to religion often retain a deep appreciation for the spiritual. I remember talking to a gay man once who denounced the Church bitterly but said he was sorry he couldn't be a part of it. Gays have not rejected religion; religion has rejected them. And even without religion, they tend to have deep spiritual sensitivity.

The usefulness of this "sprituality" is obvious. Gay men, if they can overcome their antipathy to organized religion (which has treated them so unkindly), can be natural spiritual leaders whose attraction and sensitivity to the spiritual makes them perfect guides for others. They not only are sensitive to the presence and importance of the transcendent but are adept at making it present in the finite, which leads us to our final characteristic.

Creativity. Gay men are stereotypically (if often not kindly) noted for their creativity; for whatever reasons, they seem able not only to perceive beauty and the transcendent but also to translate it into art, music, drama, and liturgy. Matthew Fox discusses that ability, and says it results, first, from what he calls the *via negativa*, or the process of letting go of parents, families, and self-archetypes so early in life as they come out. That emptying out, the low self-image that sometimes results from growing up gay, and the fact that homosexuals do not have families of their own into which to direct their energy (to which I have already alluded), leads to a different kind of generativity, the *via creativa*. Unable to give birth to biological children, gay creativity takes another shape. Matthew Fox puts it this way: "The birthing of beauty and truth in all ways that art can do so—dance, pottery, music, poetry, drama, to name a few—is in fact the birthing of alternative children. These are the gifts the creative person wishes to leave."[5]

Ministry often involves "making something out of nothing," creating in the fullest sense of the word. Ministers must often pull hope from despair, life from death, beauty and transcendence from ordinary, earthy elements. Gay creativity, linked as it is to the spiritual, seems to have a special place here, and seems to be a resource upon which the Church has drawn heavily through the centuries.

One of the traditional justifications for clerical celibacy involved availability: the priest's availability would be curtailed if he were married and had a family to care for. While imposed celibacy carries with it problems of its own, gay people, who would not raise families in any event, seem to have a special charism for celibate ministry, at least inasmuch as they are able to direct their creative energies into channels other than biological parenthood.

My purpose in this chapter has been threefold: to illustrate the various ways in which priests are gay; to offer some reasons why so many priests are gay, or why so many gay men are attracted to ministry; and to suggest that far from being exceptions or embarrassments to priesthood, gay men are well suited to ministry and have served the Church well in this capacity for a long time.

I have, for the most part, avoided any moral judgments; in fact, some of my suggestions run counter to traditional Catholic moral teaching on homosexuality. My suggestions are pastoral and should not be understood as fulfilling the letter of current teaching on homosexuality; the moral issues involved are entirely another issue and are being dealt with at length elsewhere.

I have also tried to avoid politicizing my comments, even though I find the Church's position on homosexuality increasingly unacceptable, especially when large numbers of its own clergy are gay and are denied the pastoral help and appreciation they deserve. Though my intent in this chapter is not to start a mad dash from the closet, I hope that it will at least enable priests who are gay to face that fact honestly and responsibly and to find some measure of understanding from their friends and superiors. I also hope that the "invisible gifts" they have been bringing to ministry all along will be recognized and nurtured.

3. A Christian Spirituality

REV. T. THOMPSON

I am a religious priest and I am gay. I knew that I was gay at the age of twelve. I was attracted to my male friends and not to the girls. I felt confused and guilty. The messages that I received from parents, peers, friends, Church, and society told me that I was "odd," a "sinner," a "freak," a "fairy," a "queer." I did not know where to turn. I began to pretend. I pretended by working very hard at being like everyone else. This meant that I had to learn how to be a sneak. I had to sneak a look at the drugstore when we went through the magazine rack. My friends looked at the "girlie" magazines; I looked too, but covertly I was glancing at the "muscle men" magazines. I had to sneak my magazines home in secret and could not share them with anyone. I would wrap them around my ankle and cover them with my sock to sneak them into the house. My pretension led to isolation. While my friends were sharing their fun together I was alone with my fantasies. This aloneness bothered me the most.

As was expected, I dated girls. I was frightened most of the time, but it is misleading to say that I was frightened of women. I was not afraid of them; I was afraid that I would not be able to "perform" sexually after I heard my friends describe their encounters. I can recall my trembling as I slow-danced with my girlfriends, wondering and fearing: "What if I get too close and

Rev. T. Thompson is the pseudonym of a gay priest.

119

they begin to get excited? What can I possibly do?" I can remember taking these girls "parking" and pretending that I was turned on. I would fantasize about one of my male friends. What a horrible game! I think the girls knew.

Literally, I was attracted to the boy next door. My fantasies became fulfilled in our wrestling matches. I was infatuated with him and would wait for him to come home from school so that we could wrestle. Eventually, during the struggle, I would become aroused and have an orgasm, and the match would end. I can still remember the smell of his cologne.

As I entered the seminary I was a very frightened and angry person. I felt isolated because of my sexual orientation. Yet I sensed that God was calling me to serve as an ordained minister in the Church. Of course, the all-male environment of the seminary frightened me even more, and I began to ask, "Will I be able to control my impulses? Will I be attracted to someone who lives in the same room with me? How will I avoid the possibilities if the urges arise?" Fear and sexual attraction were closely linked in my psyche. The new environment only reinforced this development and continued to nurture the curiosity and the fear. Which feeling would prove to be more powerful? On one level I was hoping to be attracted to another seminarian, and on the other I knew that I would be expelled if I ever acted on this attraction.

I can remember living close to a few seminarians who were openly gay. In fact, two were lovers who slept together every night just down the hall. I never became close to these two. I feared that becoming too close to t m might cause me to be contaminated by association. If and when they were found out I too might be suspect. This fear prevented me from establishing a friendship that might have helped me to face myself. It kept me from a closer relationship with those who would accept me.

This type of fear, it seems to me, was typical for gay seminarians. We wanted desperately to be accepted by those in authority, and we feared their rejection because it would prevent us from realizing our goal of priesthood. In the process, we failed to establish relationships with our own peers. There was a certain underlying knowledge among us. We all suspected each other's sexual curiosity. We lived in dread that another might discover it for sure and reveal it to the superiors. So we learned to fear even ourselves, and my fear kept me pretending even more strongly than before.

I began to take on a role that communicated a lack of need for others. I developed a personality that was constantly in a position to help other people. I pretended to be "straight" and condemned those who were effeminate or "questionable" in their sexuality. The intense inferiority that I felt and that was reinforced by the culture led me to desire to be superior and perfect. As my defense I led others to believe that I was stronger, holier, more mature and whole than they. I led others to see me as someone who could not be hurt, who would not become overemotional, who was always in charge. I was the person who had all the answers. The seminarians would come to me with their many and varied problems and anxieties, and I would give advice and counsel. It worked because it fit in so beautifully with the model of the priesthood as a helping profession.

I chose to pretend to be the "good seminarian" doing exactly what was expected of me and obeying all the rules. I knew just when to be present in chapel so that I could be seen and praised. I knew where to go on retreat so that I could gain the respect of the faculty and administration. I knew the type of spirituality to show forth so that I would be applauded. I knew just how hard to study so that I could be considered intelligent. I knew which social causes to join in order to please the seminary staff. I was accepted and promoted, but I did not have any inner peace.

Much of what I did to create this defense mechanism was not undertaken consciously, of course. My actions did not stem from bad will. I actually thought that I was living maturely and responsibly. In reality, I lacked integrity. Pretending had not changed the reality of who I was.

This phony way of life did have its petty rewards: I belonged to the group. The problem is that I did not belong to myself, so even the collective belonging was hypocritical. There was no "I" to belong, so the group was cheated. This reward was not worth the price, because deep down I knew that I was only being accepted for a lie and a facade. It was an unholy belonging because it was not authentic. It was irrational because it was based mostly on feelings that were out of control. I criticized many people and made them look foolish, all in the name of my own insecurity.

This same fear and insecurity pushed my anger into wrath. I remember, while still in the seminary, working as an associate to a hospital chaplain. We lived in the same apartment complex and had developed a close and friendly relationship. One night, after a party at which we were all drinking, this chaplain came to my bedroom and got in bed with me. I remember being incensed and physically throwing him out of bed. How dare he presume that I would want to sleep with him! I was violent with this man, my "friend," and from that point on would not have anything to do with him. I stopped working there, even though I liked the ministry a great deal, and after the incident, even when he and I met, I would refuse to talk with him or recognize his presence. This is anger pushed to wrath. I had a desire for vengeance and can remember telling others of the incident and ridiculing this chaplain in front of them. All the time, I knew that I, too, was gay and that I had missed a great chance to show compassion. I sinned. I rejected my friend but, even more, rejected myself. The alienation had its effects on both of us.

Finally, with an utter crash that came from God, I reached such a point of fear, depression, and curiosity that I could not live with the deception any longer. My face hit the mud in utter desperation and depression; I hit bottom. I was tricked, through my anger at self, into needing others. I discovered a friend.

The grace that God offers sometimes has a sneaky way of

getting through. God can trick us. My pretending eventually led to a great deal of personal and emotional turmoil. Thank God for this great gift! I was forced to my knees, where I had to face my own self with my weakness and brokenness. One day, after I had been shut up in my bedroom for hours listening to mournful music in the dark, a priest who was living with me came to my door, knocked, opened the door, sat down, and began to talk with me.

He asked me what was wrong, why I was locked away like this. I didn't respond, because I was afraid and didn't trust him. He continued the conversation by asking me if I was gay. "What!" I said. He continued by explaining that he had just dealt with his own gayness while away at school and had been wondering if I was dealing with the same issue. He recognized the symptoms, he said, and wanted to know if he could be of any help. Normally, my pride and fear would have prevented me from responding. But I could feel the yes screaming inside me, and somehow it came out of my mouth. What relief I felt! We talked for a long time, and he shared his life and feelings and invited the same response from me. It reminds me now of how God deals with us. God first shares our life, in Jesus, and then invites us to respond.

This man was the first real experience, in the flesh, that I ever had of God. I had firmly believed that God would only accept me if I rejected my homosexuality, so strong had been the conditioning from church and society. Now, through this man's intimate sharing, I discovered that God's love is all-embracing, accepting my gayness along with all of me. This experience became the basis for my new spirituality. This new spirituality reappraised what was real sin in my life and what were the most important Christian attitudes and values for me to focus on. I had found my first true friend and learned, through experience, what compassion is. In the recognition of my need for help and the rejection of my pride I discovered the grace of life.

Integrity

The cornerstone of my spirituality became integrity. So much of Christian morality is focused on external actions, whether thought, word, or deed: I have a bad thought; I say a bad word; I do a bad deed. We develop an elaborate ethic to avoid evil and do good, but it really remains external to us. We can be kind, considerate, helpful, self-sacrificing people, yet the inner person is not developing, and we do not become any closer to God. In fact, at times, these very acts of charity can keep us away from God, because they are keeping us from facing our own true selves. The real sin that is there we run away from, either through denying that it exists, projecting it onto another person, or some similar psychological mechanism. This avoidance is why gay people who are afraid of their own homosexuality so often suffer from homophobia and are the very ones who persecute gays. Rather than live on this external level, then, one needs to look more deeply into the interior spirit by which one lives.

Spirituality is a style of life. Prior to my experience with this friend, my life was one of deception. Now, for the first time, I was able to discover God in and through compassion and intimacy. I was able to understand more clearly how compassion and intimacy are at the very root of my faith.

In every way of life we are presented with choices. God gives each of us the opportunity to choose the spirit by which we are going to live. We can choose the spirit of arrogance, the spirit of competition, the spirit of sex, the spirit of power, the spirit of fear. The list can go on indefinitely. Each of these choices forms a spirituality.

In my life, I chose a spirit of status coming from the priesthood. I believed that priesthood would make me acceptable to myself and others, so I did all that I could to become and remain a priest, even if it meant self-deception, isolation, and hiddenness. I do not blame priesthood but only myself for the choice. The call was there and still is there, but desire for priesthood replaced the Spirit of God and led me to live hypocritically, dishonestly, and irresponsibly. I lost my integrity.

The spirit of integrity is the fundamental gift. In traditional spiritual literature it might be called humility. Whatever the name, without it there is no growth in the Spirit, no coming closer to God. The search for our integrity means that at times we must stand against the generally accepted norms in order to discover the truth.

For example, in traditional spirituality we are taught to try to control our sexual thoughts and actions outside of marriage because they would violate the sixth and ninth commandments. In reality, it seems to me it is far better to have the thoughts and even to act upon them in certain circumstances rather than suppress them and never discover the truth of who you are. Going to pornographic movies might be a very graced thing to do if it helps one to discover the truth about self. Purity, in its precise meaning, is integrity and wholeness. Never allowing oneself a "dirty thought" could be real impurity if it meant that one was running away from inner truth. In making integrity the fundamental issue we can take seriously Jesus' saying, "You shall know the truth and the truth shall set you free."

After speaking with my friend and admitting the truth about my own homosexuality I was led to places like gay bars and adult bookstores. I say "was led" because I firmly believed that it was the Spirit of God drawing me to accept and deal with this reality. Although I no longer find the need to frequent these places (most gay males do not), I did discover God in these dark inner sanctums. Here, I was compelled to face my own fears and my own self. I was driven by the Spirit of God to face the truth.

In our concentration upon external actions as a basis for morality, we have also given a great deal of attention to genital sex. In my many visits to gay bars, I rarely had genital sex with anyone. In fact, in the twelve years I have admitted the truth about myself, admitted being gay, I have rarely had genital sex with anyone. Somehow, we are led to believe that people have sex all the time. In fact, people rarely have genital sex compared to the many other activities of life. This is true of married couples and is true of gay people. The real point in asceticism is not the external action but the internal motivation. Genital sex can be morally evil when it uses another person for personal gratification. I have done this, but rarely. It is not the central issue in understanding sexuality. The truth about going to gay bars is that gay people can find the acceptance and understanding in these places that is so lacking in church and society.

Compassion

The second fundamental truth of my spirituality, flowing out of self-acceptance, became compassion. Compassion is the ability to identify with, to sense our oneness with, to suffer with, the rest of humanity. In my experience there are two important elements that bring it out. First, because I was rejected and ridiculed for an essential part of my human nature I was able to begin to understand more deeply the pain and suffering of others, just as my friend, having gone through this experience himself, was able to suffer with me.

I have been able to see this compassion at work in my own life over these past twelve years. I no longer see myself as being so self-righteous and judgmental. Many priests have come to me during this time to discuss their sexuality. These discussions have revealed many varying and idiosyncratic sexual desires, drives, and fantasies.[1] I cannot sit in judgment over any of these men, because I have experienced the great pain of a self-righteous attitude myself.

Second, since most people would still consider unhealthy and unnatural what I have come to consider a positive part of my personality, my homosexuality, I began to accept the ambiguity of life. I am less and less threatened by the differences and changes in God's creation. A secure identity is not threatened by differences, does not need to attack and does not need to be defensive. I can now say that my way and my culture are not the supreme standard for all of humanity. I can accept people for who they are, without any need to try to change them, no matter how "odd" or "freaky" they might seem. Humility might be defined as this ability to live with ambiguity. As I grow in acceptance of my own ambiguous being I am humbled because I am not everything that I want to be. In this experience I am also learning that others are not necessarily going to be what I want them to be. I can begin to feel as comfortable in the presence of a prostitute as in the presence of the pope.

Intimacy

The third formative experience that flowed from this encounter with my friend and is basic to my spirituality is intimacy. Erik Erickson, commonly considered to be the psychologist who introduced intimacy as an important life value, defines it as "the capacity to commit one's self to concrete affiliations and partnerships and to develop the ethical strength to abide by such commitments even though they may call for significant compromises and sacrifices."[2]

Intimacy is the relationship two people have with each other that enables them to share deep concerns, honest feelings, and personal desires. It is a disposition that is open to being helped and loved. It is power through vulnerability. It means that a person will not set objectives and goals in life in isolation, that decisions will not be made independently but will be made in conjunction with the other who is trusted and who understands. It is an interdependence that involves being as receptive as an open vessel for new input and new information. Intimacy finds its antithesis in fixed and static opinions.

Prior to the acceptance and compassion of my friend, I was unable to be intimate. I was unapproachable. I can remember, in fact, many occasions when I would physically recoil if someone got too close to me. I was cynical and saw most relationships as selfish. And I saw work and ministry as the only important things in life; I was a workaholic running from the inner truth.

Intimacy is a basic human need; it is not an option! Without intimacy I was living a distorted life. Celibate people can live healthy lives if they have intimacy. Without intimacy, celibacy can have many psychopathological effects.

I believe that gay priests and religious have a better opportunity to express and receive intimacy because the Church expects and encourages us to live in same-sex environments in our communities and rectories. Two gay men who have accepted their sexuality could develop a deep relationship of cooperation, encouragement, self-sacrifice, commitment, compromise, and ethical strength. This relationship could make a marvelous contribution to life and ministry in the church. Certainly this has all been true in my relationship with my friend. I believe that it has also been true in the history of the Church.

With intimacy we can come to experience the ultimate love of enemies; we can grow to love those who hate us by coming to love ourselves just as we are. The more we are able to accept ourselves, the better able we are to accept others, even enemies, because we have accepted our own inner enemies and darkness.

Intimacy involves physical touch that is sought; one feels a desire to be physically close. People often confuse this with genital sex. The fear of genital sex, however, is probably one of the greatest causes of promiscuity. When we respond to another out of a fear of genital sex, we can be driven by forces that are compelling and impulsive, negative forces that can lead us to do the very things that we hate. For example, when I first went into a gay bar I was trembling with fear, overcome by this force. After entering and finding a place at a table with some others I began to become very flirtatious. My inhibitions and fears were so strong that I went to the other extreme to relieve them. This can happen with genital sex. It is a true paradox of human life. Inner isolation can be the root cause of unwanted genital activity. Somehow, many people feel that if they do not discuss its possibility beforehand then they are not responsible if something happens. If I had admitted my fear to the people in that bar we would have had a much different experience. Openness about sex and about honest feelings can relieve the extreme tension that might bring about the opposite of what one intends. Communication of the truth leads to co-responsibility.

I recall a priest who came to me once seeking help because he was sexually attracted to a close friend who was also a priest. The two men were living together but were not lovers. They did, however, share many things in common and enjoyed each other's company. The man who came to me was not conscious of his sexual attraction to his friend for some time. At first he thought that the attraction was merely "platonic" in that they had so much in common. Suddenly, however, he began to have sexual fantasies about his friend and realized that he had more than just a social relationship. The men were now beginning to draw apart. They would become angry with each other over small things, and both were becoming petty and adolescent. They were slowly moving away from each other, no longer sharing life and doing things in common. I asked this man if he would invite his friend to the next session with me. He did this. Over a period of time it surfaced that both men were physically and sexually attracted to each other and were both afraid to discuss it. When they were eventually able to discuss their true feelings the anger subsided, and they could both begin to take responsibility for their relationship and to make responsible choices.

Intimacy involves a willingness to be honest with each other insofar as possible and an ability to enter into conflict without fear of rejection. Fears and negative emotions can be openly discussed.

I spent many years running from this type of intimacy. I believe that many gay people do the same. I ran because I sexualized feelings of attraction and intimacy, and in this fear of genital involvement I missed the opportunity for intimate relationship. I kept these potential relationships at a distance.

This sexualization can have harmful effects on anyone. Our society places rigid restrictions on warm associations between people of the same sex, especially men. Because of this, many of these feelings are repressed or are conveyed through a tough, angry, macho exterior. Participation in sporting events, for example, can give men in our culture a way to express warm feelings. It can be very acceptable on a football field for one player to embrace another after the touchdown, and it is unobjectionable for hockey players to hug and kiss each other after a goal is scored. Baseball players can slap one another on the "butt," and we don't sexualize these actions, or men can go to the local bar and, after a few drinks, begin to embrace one another. We seem able to accept these varieties of physical intimacy because they are in the context of the male, macho subculture. As long as there is some type of rough or "strong" behavior that accompanies this touch it seems acceptable, and reference to sexuality is shunned.

This message was clear to me when I was young and just beginning to experience my sexuality. Wrestling with my friend was an acceptable way to touch and to get affection. It became a way for me to receive physical, sexual gratification.

Men tend to sexualize their feelings in this society when they simply want warm, intimate association with one another. These sexualized tensions, anxieties, and stresses lead to anger that can be projected onto gay people. Attraction can lead to repulsion when fear rules. People tend to affirm this sexualization and then become preoccupied with it; the end result is called *homophobia*, a term often used to describe hostile reactions to lesbians and gay men. It implies a one-dimensional construct of attitudes that express irrational fears.[3]

My experience with other gay priests and religious is that they often have the strongest homophobia. I believe that this is also true of many bishops and religious superiors. It is so, I think, because these people feel that they have so much at stake. As it was with me in the seminary, the security, power, and status of priesthood overrides the truth. The homophobia can become so conditioned that it is unconscious.

I am speaking primarily of the defensive type of homophobia. What can oftentimes underlie fear, it seems to me, is simply a need for warm, close, physical touch from another man. Sexualization of this need can complicate relationships with others because the norm in our society is to interpret this need for warmth, closeness, and intimacy as a feminine characteristic. The resulting prejudice is that only women can engage in this type of intimacy and caring and closeness: the classic masculine/feminine stereotypes that are being questioned today.

I believe that I can have good relationships with both women and men. I have no need to compete with other men for the responses of women; therefore, I believe that I can relate with women on a more equal basis. The competitive spirit derives from male aggression. Biologically it is closely linked to sexuality. Aggression and competition can stem from male sexual desire for women and from a desire for sexual release.

Moreover, being gay and having endured the pain of self-acceptance brings me to experience a certain vulnerability that I do not believe is available to many men in our society. Feelings such as gentleness, receptivity, and vulnerability are not generally acceptable for men in our culture. It seems to me, however, that cooperation and vulnerability are two of the hallmarks of ministry and religion, especially in Christianity.

Because I am gay, I have no need to shun relationships with other men. I can show affection, can touch, and can have intimacy with men. I believe this is a real gift. Again, the general attitude of our society tells us that feelings of attraction for someone of the same sex are repulsive, and these attitudes become ingrained in individuals and the community. I do not have the homophobia that can prevent close relationships with men.

Intimacy enables us to confront inner darkness because it gives strength for self-acceptance. When we know that another loves us and accepts us we are strengthened to accept our own being. We do not need to force people to accept us through power and control. I sometimes fear that this is the "way" of the gay rights movement. My fear is that such movements often create further alienation and oppression. Acceptance cannot be forced. Very often, coercion is a way for men in our society to receive acceptance, through competitive business dealings and competitive sports and also through competitive preaching, teaching, or pastoring.

Gay spirituality can incorporate a type of intimacy that is capable of sharing deep concerns, honest feelings, and personal desires, an ability to express limitations and weaknesses, a disposition that is open to being helped and loved. Intimacy is a type of relationship that invites challenges and does not struggle after power; it is not enabled by competition and jealousy; it can go beyond this competitive strife. It is power through vulnerability.

I believe that gay people can begin to break patterns of sexualization and homophobia. Men who find themselves closely together might go through the following pattern of sexualized feelings:

Comfort. Initially, two men who like each other will spend time together and feel comfortable in each other's presence. They will do things in common and become social friends.

Attraction. After some time, these two men begin to become conscious of being attracted to each other, or at least one to the other. This appeal and allurement can lead to desire.

Desire. One or both of the men has homosexual feelings and begins to desire the other, either physically or emotionally, or both. This is usually where rationalization and projection can enter the picture. This is also where honesty and openness are paramount—the truth, these feelings need to be shared with the other. Obviously, this attraction can often remain in the unconscious; hence, we can find ourselves "acting out" when under the influence of alcohol or drugs. When people recover from the intoxication they may not "remember."

Fear. If the feelings are not expressed, we can see the emergence of defensive homophobia. This strong and irrational fear can lead to a denial of the fantasies.

Sexualization. Out of fear, one person may begin to blame the other for becoming too close and wanting sex. These feelings can cause a great deal of harm because they are often conveyed to a third party. In the priesthood and religious life they are often told to the superior.

Opposition. Here, the person who sexualized the feelings distances himself from the other and begins to see the other as "untouchable." He may also communicate this message to others, who will begin to have similar feelings.

Withdrawal. Others begin to avoid the accused person. Thus, groups of people who may have previously been friendly begin to shun the other party for being "queer" or a "fag."

Anger. Arising from the segregation, anger can turn into wrath and push the person into total isolation and cause him to feel resentment and bitterness.

Tension. Rising frustration becomes so strong that it causes a break in relationships, not only between these two men but also between the one man and the community.

Repulsion. Disgust, hate, and horror lead to isolation for the gay person. The alienation is complete.

The original feelings are repressed and often result in defensive projection. The original feelings, however, are quite normal. We need to ask for the grace of greater consciousness of feelings so that we can make authentic moral choices. Intense and irrational fear might be the primary clue to what is actually happening inside. Fantasized fear is the basis for homophobia.

Intimacy means that a person is mature and able to discern and take responsibility. In order to do this, however, one must first of all admit the truth, and this means the truth about feelings and thoughts. Authentic moral discernment cannot take place without this step. In the pattern just discussed, the original feelings of attraction and of having common bonds needed to be discussed openly. If this were to happen, then the relationship could proceed on a more honest basis and might have a better chance of survival.

Positive Asceticism

That I have gained these insights does not mean that I have arrived. I have discovered in all this the need for real discipline in self-acceptance and disclosure of the truth. In the past our discipline has been seen merely as a need to curtail instincts. Though this can be part of discipline, I have come to believe that self-revelation in truth is a much more important form of discipline. This self-revelation is a genuine asceticism.

Normally, one thinks of asceticism in terms of controlling and disciplining passions. Fasting from food and drink so as to learn to control the physical appetites would be an example. But dying to false images and idols of ourselves is also a real asceticism, one that requires a great deal of practice before it is mastered.

The temptation to fall into the old ways occurs over and over again. I have had to learn to recognize this self-rejection when it begins to creep in. I become fearful and almost phobic. I begin to feel anxiety, wondering who might discover my inner truth. For example, I can be at a party and suddenly begin wondering if others there might think that I am gay. I especially begin to feel this fear if I am attracted to someone at the party. Because of my fear, I will hold back from engaging this attractive person in conversation, thinking that he might wonder if I am "coming on" to him. By doing this, I once again isolate myself in my own little inner proud world, fixed on my own self, living in my fantasy world. Or, I might keep my attention fixed upon someone else, particularly someone who is explicitly gay, and start mentally, or even verbally, to denigrate that person so as to build up myself. Both are serious forms of pride, which is the root of sin.

A positive asceticism is called for so that we can learn the discipline of discrimination, which means becoming sensitive to ourselves and others and beginning to take responsibility. We need to be able to make distinctions. What are my real feelings toward another person of the same sex? What is imagined about these feelings? What feelings does the other person seem to be having? How aware are the two people of the messages that are being conveyed between them? What is being said with words and body? What is being communicated? What is the context? Answering such questions takes real discipline: to listen to the verbal and nonverbal messages, to hear the ideas, to see the interpersonal situation, to understand the possible differences in culture and subculture, to notice group processes, to be aware of cultural trends. Messages given by two people always have implications. We are responsible for our own actions. Lack of awareness can be an excuse for not taking responsibility, and people can choose to block awareness by using drugs, alcohol, and/or defense mechanisms like rationalization.

The more we are conscious of ourselves the greater our ability to accept the truth. This is a key element in any spirituality. For example, what is happening in my body when I am with another person? What are my sexual reactions? It is foolish to deny that they are present because they are present in every encounter. Is there arousal? Is there repulsion? Is the heart rate increasing? Is there a blush on the face? Is there anxiety or fear? Everyone has signs of attraction, and we all need to become aware of what these are. We also need to become more sensitive to what is happening in another. Only then can the truth be discovered. Moreover, even if there is sexual attraction it does not necessarily mean that any physical, sexual, genital action must take place. If this were the case we would have general chaos! On the contrary, we will be in greater control of ourselves when we admit the truth and then take responsibility for ourselves. Feelings, even feelings of sexual attraction, are not actions! We need to learn to distinguish and discriminate. This requires self-discipline.

Priests and religious need to learn how to understand and interact in social situations. If one becomes aware during a social situation that another person is becoming too close in terms of sexual activity, then one needs to make a response in freedom.

Seduction is an activity that needs to be better understood. Seduction, in the sense of allurement and enticement, is very powerful, and we can entice in many ways: at a party or in the pulpit, after mass or in the classroom, out to dinner or in a counseling session. Seduction can use words, tone of voice, pitch, body language, and ritualistic actions.[4] This behavior can be confusing because we may use it unconsciously, perhaps because we are lonely or need affirmation or see it as affirming others. Also, it can be rationalized into a form of piety (e.g., many of us have been taught to be "nice" to everyone and to see this as a spiritual gift, or, we may rationalize our need for touch into a healing ceremony or see it as a helping technique). People do not always interpret our messages the way we intend. Just as we cannot be seduced unless we choose to respond, we cannot totally blame others when they respond to our enticement.

Gay people can feel an overpowering need to be wanted, accepted, and approved because of the strong rejection expressed by church and society. This need can lead us to be easily seduced, indeed, can be a cause of the promiscuity that many people in religious circles are concerned about. This conflict can bring us to lead a double life: during the day we are people pleasers, doing what is expected, and at night we are trying to find acceptance and approval through sexual encounters with strangers. Society can create the very thing it hates by forcing people into subcultures through rejection and ridicule. When we experience enough rejection we become dehumanized and no longer treat ourselves or others with respect. This can provide a basis for promiscuity.

Anonymous genital encounters do not enhance self-acceptance. If we can experience intimacy we can be led toward greater self-respect and away from anonymous genital gratification. Obviously, anonymous encounters and promiscuity cannot satisfy the longing for intimacy. But unless we begin to admit the truth about ourselves we may adopt this compulsive life-style.

A Christian Way of Life

Out of all this, I believe, we can find a basis for a Christian spirituality. These three experiences, integrity, compassion, and intimacy, were paramount in the life and ministry of Jesus.

The Scriptures verify that God has taken the first step of revelation and self-disclosure. The Christian God is Emmanuel. God participates in our humanity, shares our ways of relating, our loves and joys, our pains and sorrows, our securities and doubts, our isolation and death. In my own life, my friend came into that darkened room and reminded me of how God deals with us. God first shares in our life, in Jesus, and then invites us to reopen.

I cannot predict the paradoxes and changes of life. One day I can experience faith and another doubt; one time fear and another time hope, dreams and regrets, anger and stillness, pain and pleasure, acceptance and rejection, strength and weakness. Some days I can experience all of this and more! God is present in all of this ambiguity, and God alone can enter into this intricacy. God is Emmanuel and can be with me in any and every experience of life. As I experience joy, God can be loving Mother/Father. When I experience doubt God can be absent. When I experience depression God is the Suffering Servant. Anger can bring me to experience Jesus throwing the money changers out of the Temple. My dreams bring me to experience the Spirit of Pentecost. When I experience forgiveness God is the father of the prodigal. When I am in need of discipline God is the message to the rich young man. Suffering can bring me to encounter God on the Cross; nurturance can bring an experience of the Last Supper and freedom an experience of the Resurrection. I experience myself as being gay, and God is friend and lover. As I know myself and admit the complex truth in self-revelation, I am known by God, and I grow in the power of Christian integrity.

Jesus spoke and acted out of his own integrity. He did not teach as the other rabbis and authorities; he was not authoritarian and did not need to quote the other rabbis and ancient commentaries to prove a point. (We are reminded by contemporary psychology that authoritarian personalities are usually very insecure.) The Scribes and Pharisees, of course, saw this as heresy. The teaching of Jesus is entirely new. Jesus' authority came from a unique relationship with God, and Jesus discovered a power and a treasure that is unequaled. This is the Spirit of Jesus. We, too, are given the grace to speak and act out of our own integrity. The ministry of Jesus gives us the meaning of compassion. Biblical scholars tell us about the elements of this mission. We are called to follow it.

First of all, the reign of God is central in the focus of Jesus. Here is the description of that reign as Jesus saw it:

The Spirit of the Lord is upon me, because the Lord has anointed me; he has sent me to bring glad tidings to the lowly, to heal the brokenhearted, to proclaim liberty to captives and release to the prisoners, to announce a year of favor from the Lord and a day of vindication by our God, to comfort all who mourn, to place on those who mourn in Zion a diadem instead of ashes, to give them oil of gladness instead of mourning, a glorious mantle instead of a listless spirit. They will be called oaks of justice, planted by the Lord to show his glory. (Isaiah 61:1–3)

We are called to bring glad tidings to the lowly, to heal the brokenhearted, to proclaim liberty to captives and release to prisoners. This reign is the threshold of Christian life as we, too, yearn for the experience of being lowly, poor, broken-hearted, and imprisoned. Being gay in this culture and church can enable us to experience compassion. Being gay can be the threshold of the reign of God.

Jesus did not live or preach or teach in fear of what others might think or do. We, too, need not be tempered by what others might think of homosexuality or by their fear of it. It is a gift that can be shared with others who are suffering, poor, brokenhearted, lowly, and imprisoned. Freedom can bring us to help others to be released from their bigotry and prejudice so that God's healing light can shine on all. The integrity and authority of Jesus is compassion.

It is a call to suffer with our enemies, with those who condemn and hate us. This is the only love that can transform hatred for gay people into acceptance. It is a transcending and transforming love, a love that can convert the world, a love that can break down all barriers and fears, open all prisons and heal all brokenness. Our gayness can be a way in which we experience this prejudice, fear, and imprisonment, and this experience of brokenness can bring compassion.

Jesus had a unique intimacy with God. From the experience of Jesus we know that God loves all people equally without exception and without bigotry and prejudice. This intimacy is the only real strength and can give us the courage to confront the darkness and evil within: the pride of self-righteousness, the power that wants to see self as better than others, the authority that condemns rather than forgives and the great darkness that projects evil onto others as a way of escaping it inside oneself.

Being gay has within it the seeds of integrity, compassion, and intimacy. With the help of grace, we can live in honesty and integrity. We can suffer with one another. We can then try to suffer with our enemies. This, indeed, can be the hallmark of a gay Christian spirituality. Being gay has the potential spark of compassion built into it.

My life thus has taught me that an experience of intimacy can bring integrity and compassion to light. These three values interact with one another in a great dynamic that is both humanly healthy and spiritually sustaining. Integrity, compassion, and intimacy form the basis for a truly Christian religious experience. If we can allow them to be enflamed, we can have an experience of God.

4. The Fears of a Gay Priest

REV. R. ROBERTS

It was the funeral of an eighty-four-year-old black man named Willie that provided me with the categories to identify my fears as a gay priest. Willie had outlived all his blood relatives and friends. He died a pauper and a ward of the state. He had been a compulsive gambler, a heavy smoker and drinker, and an inconsistent worker.

I first met Willie at a VA hospital. He was paralyzed by strokes and in pain from cancer. In preparing the homily for his Mass of Christian burial I was drawn to the Scripture: " 'When did we visit you when you were ill or in prison?' The king will answer them: 'I assure you, as often as you did it for one of my least brothers, you did it for me' "(Matthew 25:39–40). I reflected on the contrast of values. Our culture and society offer rewards to those who are young, bright, good-looking, and competitive. All the others must fend for themselves. But it is the revelation of Jesus that the kingdom of God belongs to the least, the last, the lost, and the lonely.

As I was preaching this message I was trying to give a word of hope to the three people who had come to mourn Willie. As the sermon proceeded, I realized that I was also preaching for myself. For I too felt among the least, the last, the lost, and the lonely. Though I was well-educated, financially secure, white, and half Willie's age, I was a priest who had just come to realize

Rev. R. Roberts is the pseudonym of a gay priest.

that I am truly a homosexual. This fact would make much of society, and even the Church, refer to me as abnormal or perverted, a man with an evil inclination.

It was a fear-filled realization. In a statement by the ten black Catholic bishops of the United States there is a challenging indictment that could be used to describe my fear.

There is evidence that just as some white Americans continue to feel that to have black neighbors, black co-workers and black classmates will be disruptive of their value system and their familiar patterns of life, some white Catholics feel that it will be equally disruptive to share the Scriptures, the Bread of Life and Cup of Eternal Salvation with black Catholics.

As a result, when white Catholics pass through black neighborhoods they may feel sorry for black people, feel afraid of them, or even feel guilty about their plight, but they do not welcome the call of the Spirit to invite their black sisters and brothers to the Tables of the Lord. Consequently, many black Americans still feel unwelcome in the Catholic church.[1]

I read that statement and substituted "straight" for "white" and "gay or lesbian" for "black." I then asked myself, "Would you choose to be gay?" My response was instant: "Oh, God, no! Why would I choose to be among the rejected; the least, the last, the lost, the lonely?"

I grew up in a conservative German, half-Catholic, half-Lutheran home in which the stress was on the mind and the will, the powers that set us above the beast, a home in which touching was a tinder that could spark an evil passion unleashed by Adam's sin. Adolescence became a curse. I remember the priest who came to our eighth-grade classroom one day, separated the boys from the girls as a shepherd separates sheep from goats, and proceeded to give us boys the shocking sex talk. He drew two penises on the blackboard, one in a flacid state, the other erect. "That," he said, pointing to the first, "is no sin; but this one is a *mortal* sin." I became a puberty-stricken lad who dutifully went to confession weekly thereafter.

This fear of sex plagued me for years and would not be resolved until I was in my mid-thirties. In the meantime I had many experiences that would intensify this stress.

In high school my most difficult time came during gym class. The smell of sweating bodies and the sight of naked male adolescents sent me into a sexual fantasy craving explanation, understanding, and guidance. I never thought of myself in terms of being a homosexual. At the time I thought my strong sexual attraction to the guys was simply due to being in an all-boys high school. For me it seemed to be a matter of just growing up. I figured that someday in the future I would feel the way the other guys did toward girls. I dated girls throughout high school, but I was never sexually attracted to them. I limited my dating to the usual social events: Halloween, Thanksgiving, Christmas, Valentine's Day, the prom, and so on. I managed most of the time to join other couples. The eight guys I hung around with were not all that girl-crazy either. We enjoyed sitting together and cheering until we were hoarse at the football and basketball games, working on the school newspaper, serving Mass, participating in the Sodality, and playing cards. At the twenty-fifth anniversary of our high school graduation I discovered that all but one were homosexuals! As the saying goes, "You could have fooled me."

My decision to enter the seminary after high school was based on a number of positive reasons. In my junior year I was quite involved with the Sodality. One of the brothers from the faculty used for his weekly instruction the booklet "Jesus in the Gospels," which gave a chronological portrait of Jesus based on the four Gospels. Through this experience I developed a deep personal relationship with Jesus. I felt that I knew Jesus and that he knew me. I remember the impact of the scene in which Jesus, after he had spoken of himself as the bread of life, asked the Twelve: "Do you want to leave me too?" Simon Peter answered him, "Lord, to whom shall we go? You have the words of eternal life. We have come to believe; we are convinced that you are God's holy one" (John 6:68). I was deeply impressed with the religious at school and the diocesan priests at the parish. I wanted to make my life worthwhile by helping and serving others as they were doing. I felt a call to be a parish priest. In a graduating class of 205, there were 32 who took the entrance exam for the seminary! Obviously, vocations were "in." I felt proud and sure of myself. Outside of occasional bouts of masturbation, I entered the seminary with confidence and anticipation.

At the end of the first semester at the seminary college I realized how attached I was to my parents. I missed them terribly. I was homesick! But there was little time allowed in the seminary formation to deal with real-life issues like loneliness, intimacy, sexual feelings, identity, and integration. As seminarians we were carefully and effectively isolated and controlled. The atmosphere and regulations of the seminary were hardly geared toward personal growth and maturity. Even as the Second Vatican Council was in session, we could not leave the premises, use the telephone, or make a doctor's appointment without written and verbal permission. Authorization was given only after interrogation. There was one newspaper, pinned up on a bulletin board, and one television set for a student body of three hundred. Cassocks were to be worn at all times, even on the ball fields and to the showers. All textbooks and classes in theology were in Latin; all lights were turned off by 10:00 P.M.; and all doors of students' rooms were left open for inspection during the 6:00 A.M. daily Solemn High Mass. The major concerns were academic excellence, rule keeping, and having the "right attitude." Ordination became the supreme goal to which were attached many rights and privileges. To get ordained became a way to prove one's faith, perseverance, and calling. The seminary administration and faculty were surrogate parents who were charged with rearing obedient and like-minded servants. I remember the portly seminary rector, dressed formally in his red-buttoned cassock with shoulder cape and tassled cummerbund, addressing the entire student body before lunch to issue a "monitum" (warning) against the book *Counseling the Catholic*, written by two Jesuits, Frs. Haggemeier and Gleason. These men dared to state that masturbation might not always be mortally sinful. All copies of their book were to be brought to the rector's office by that evening. We were warned against particular friendships among both seminarians and nonseminarians, men and women. Through all this repression I was allowing myself to be set up for a long-delayed sexual confrontation and integration.

I spent the first ten years in the priesthood working two jobs. Not only was I the only assistant priest in three successive parishes of 1,200 to 1,400 families but I was also a full-time high school teacher and chairperson of a department. In my "spare" time I was expected by these pastors to take care of the high school CCD, the youth club, retreats, and all the weddings. I didn't have time to think about myself and my ever-growing fear of loneliness, intimacy, and sexual identity. But the moment of truth was about to stop me in my tracks.

I must have adopted my mother's philosophy of life. She worked incessantly at home. She cooked three hot meals a day and scrubbed, waxed, and vacuumed to the point of wearing the walls, floors, and carpet thin and bald. Her spiritual motto was *Ora et Labora*, that is, "Say your prayers, and do your work." That motto also implied keep your mouth shut and your feelings to yourself. "Don't tell me your problems," she would say on occasion, "go tell them to Jesus. I got enough of my own to worry about."

Then Mom died. With her passing I discovered the deep bond we had had. She was the very first human being I knew, and locked in that inevitable struggle for her and against her throughout my life, I wondered now how well I really had known her and how well she had known me. I came to realize after her death that I had lost an authority figure. Mom's death brought me to a crossroads. I did not have to do what she said or what I thought she would want. I didn't have to please her anymore. I was on my own. Her death caused me to ask the question, Who am I *now*? I didn't want to think about that right then, because I was terminating ten years of teaching, preparing to transfer to another parish assignment, and saying goodbye to the fifth classmate who had just announced his application for dispensation from celibacy. But the can of worms had been opened. All those fears and the anger I had conveniently tucked away and held in check with my workaholism came springing out and hit me in the face. I tried to stuff those worms back in and close the lid. Strange, all the worms wouldn't go back in.

I had just arrived at my new parish assignment when I realized that my emotional equilibrium was deteriorating. I had been holding something inside for a long time, something of which I was afraid and ashamed. I remember getting up in the early morning hours one day and quietly walking outside the rectory. I began crying. I felt a deep anger at my parents, my teachers, the seminary training, the Church, society, and finally, most vehemently, God. With tears blurring my vision and my emotions creating a migraine, I looked up at the moonlit sky and shook my fist at God, up there somewhere. My mouth was quivering so badly I couldn't form the words to express my utter desperation: "What a dirty joke to play on me, God. I hope you enjoy seeing people suffer." My whole body convulsed, my head became dizzy, my legs gave way, and I crumpled to the ground in the middle of the church parking lot.

Was this a mid-life crisis? A delayed adolescent storm? Perhaps it was, but more specifically I believe it was a birthing experience, a new awareness of myself, of my sexual identity and sexual desires, my skin hunger and craving for intimate relationship. I didn't have Mom or the seminary officials to stand over me. I felt alone, abandoned, scared, and out of control. But as I said to Willie's mourners, God came to the least, the last, the lost, and the lonely. It was time for an integration of mind with heart. It was time to deal with my sexuality and my true self.

Consistent with my upbringing, I approached the whole issue academically and intellectually. I first went to the public library, but I discovered that all the books on homosexuality were tucked away in the reference section. I left without reading a thing. I was afraid of what one of those librarians would think. So I want back a week later dressed in my Roman collar. I asked for three reference books and told the attendant that I was a counselor doing some specialized research.

My first reading was very negative. These counseling manuals were saying that homosexuality was a deviation from the norm, an arrested stage of sexual development, and that sort of thing. As far as I was concerned, this was putting me down and not fitting in with my experience. I did not feel "sick." I looked at my track record and asked myself how this experience that I was becoming aware of could be so morally bad when I was clearly a morally good person and doing so much good for other people. Why would I experience all the evidence of success and joy and love? I was finding that this gayness was not something missing in my life or an evil that was attached to me like a leech but intrinsically me, and it felt "right." The love of God and the overwhelming experience of his presence had been very real to me over the years, and this was convincing me of the goodness and giftedness of my sexual orientation.

I decided to leave the reading behind to do more direct observing. The summer after my mother's death I had the opportunity to vacation in south Florida for two weeks and "check out" some of the open gay life. I visited a gay bar, a bookstore, and a disco. I was struck with two impressions: first, I was very much attracted to the men and being with them; second, there was a subculture that was not attractive. I noticed a superficiality, a slavish conformity, a painful impersonalism, and no interest in developing strong, communicative relationships. These were not just quiet places to meet some friends and talk. I felt a frightening sense of loneliness. My "spare tire," balding head, and aversion to smoke and drugs definitely made me feel "out of it." In a sense I became more confused than ever about my identity. I wondered, "Is that all there is?" I did not think so, but I did not know where to turn. It was like going back to square one.

Shortly after this experience, a young man came to me for counseling. He wanted to know something about religious life. He revealed that he was gay and that he would like to talk to a priest or brother who was gay to find out how to put the gay and religious aspects of one's life together. That was a moment of truth for me. Psychologically, I suppose it was what is termed "countertransference." But I look back on it and see it as the experience of Damien the leper. For some years he ministered to the lepers and referred to them as "you." After discovering he also had the lesions, he began addressing them as "we."

I said to this young man, "You want to talk to a religious who is gay? Well, you're talking to one." This young fellow jumped out of his chair, hugged me, and cried tears of happiness. I couldn't give him any answers on how to deal with the two realities, but I offered him the chance to talk about our mutual journey. It was the first step in what was to become an important part of the integration process: networking with other gay men.

My relationship with this man opened doors. Through him I learned of one other priest who was gay (actually an old friend of mine!). And through this priest I learned of Communication Ministry, Inc., a Catholic organization that exists to provide "a dialogue on the relationship between personal sexuality and ministry for the purpose of building community among lesbian and gay clergy and religious."[2]

When I read in the newsletter that there was a Communication-sponsored retreat just two hundred miles away, I quickly decided to go. My intention was simply to meet other homosexual religious and priests and compare notes. I was hungry to know others walking the same road. When I pulled up to the retreat house that Monday afternoon I noticed the first four cars ahead of me had license plates from my diocese. I said to myself, "Oh my God!" I still feared being discovered. I almost turned around and left. But I said, "No, I have to trust the Lord and these people." So I walked in, and the first person I met was a priest I had known and worked with for a long time. We looked at each other and just burst out laughing.

The risk had been worth it. The books and the bars had not squared with my reality, but the stories of these men on retreat did. I discovered a common thread: the suppressed sexuality, the anger at God, the reading and bar scene investigations, the difficulty in trying to come to grips in isolation, and finally the sense of relief in this networking. We felt as though we had come to the mountaintop, and over and over again we heard ourselves saying, "It is so good to be here." When I left the retreat I felt really good about myself, that I was going to be all right, that I had a lot of growing to do but that I was taking the right steps. When I came home, I continued to get together with the religious priest who had given me that first issue of *Communications* to talk and pray, and I looked forward to the retreats to come.

The story does not end there. Accepting my sexual orientation was only half the issue. The other part was the question of intimacy and celibacy. When I was in the seminary I had no real concern about celibacy. To me it simply meant not getting married or having a family. I was not even tempted to want that. In the seminary, celibacy was a nonissue. But in my maturity I began to probe something that was deeper. I started to ask myself, "What has this promise of celibacy really meant to me?" The answer was that it had been nothing, a *sine qua non* that went with the turf and no more. I began to look at my life with a new assertiveness and realized I was incomplete. I remembered how I had plowed through the tons of administrative work and performed all the required tasks of priestly ministry with great efficiency. I enjoyed doing all these things for people because I wanted to and because I was good at it. But I wasn't getting anywhere personally. I realized that the hardest part of relationship was affection.

This was the can of worms I was so afraid to open, but open I must in order to face the full reality of myself. To get emotionally close to people scared me for two reasons: either they might get to know me as gay and reject me, or they might become so attractive that I would lose self-control. So even my first steps toward letting go and becoming more affectionate were made with a great deal of holding back, caution, and guardedness. I dared to say from the pulpit one Sunday: "I do all these things because I am good at them and enjoy them, but how many of them do I do simply out of affection for you, because I love you?" I made a public examination of conscience and asked the people to forgive me for not showing affection. The people applauded, which was both affirming and disturbing at the same time.

The toughest part of my ministry was working with engaged couples. I would see them sit there holding hands, the joy in their faces as they planned their life together, the closeness they were experiencing, and I would get depressed. Why must I feel so lonely and isolated? In my prayer I said, "Lord, this is really scaring me. I don't know where this is leading me. Heal me. Make me whole. If that means having someone special in my life, send him to me." I humorously recalled the novena my female students made to Saint Anne, grandmother to Jesus: "Dear Saint Anne, help me find a man, as soon as you can."

Into my life came Michael, another priest with diverse interests but making a similar journey of discovering his true self and integrating his sexuality. We had met on one of the Communication retreats. Through correspondence and occasional visits (we were some six hundred miles apart) we decided to make our relationship an exclusive one for personal growth and development. When we are able to visit or vacation together, we spend time in prayer, celebrate Eucharist together or attend Mass at a local Dignity chapter, dialogue about our feelings, and challenge each other professionally. We decided that we were wasting too much energy trying to defend or hide ourselves from an unaccepting world and church. We could use that energy for more positive growth. We decided to stop playing games and become committed soul partners.

Now I do not feel alone. I know that there is one other person who loves me in the purest but most human of ways. I feel a depth of understanding and completeness within. I go about my work with more energy and delight. I'm much more at ease, quicker to laugh, and better at understanding people. I get more done. The people from the parish have commented how I have changed. They like what they see. I tell them how they have helped me, and they have. But more than anything, it has been this relationship with Michael that has helped. Because of him I no longer feel like part of the least, the last, the lost, and the lonely.

Some fears still remain. If the parishioners found out, for example, that I am a homosexual, what would they do? This fear saddens me. I sense a possible alienation from the very people "whom I so love and long for . . . who are my joy, my crown, my dear ones" as Saint Paul writes (Philippians 4:1). People love me, but they don't know me completely. I cannot let myself be known for who I truly am and be loved for who I truly am. So much of what is going on inside me I cannot share with people. There is such richness now in how I experience life and how I view the world, and I have to hold that back.

To disclose my homosexual orientation to my parishioners would, to the best of my discernment, cause the following: polarization of the people for and against me; suspicion or accusation of immoral activities, especially with teens and children; a request for my removal; a need for the Ordinary to make some statement or take some action about me; a witch-hunt for other closeted priests; and continued fear in the young who are becoming aware of being gay. The risk seems far too great.

As a representative of a church that is officially denying and condemning what I believe to be true about the goodness of homosexuality and the legitimacy of homosexual activity, I have further fears. I worry about maintaining my honesty and integrity. Perhaps the tension will prove great enough in the future that I will have to leave the priesthood. Here and now I say that the gospel is more than just sexual morality. That is a relatively minor part of its teaching. There is a movement toward greater openness in the Church, greater sophistication in understanding the teaching authority of the Church, more demand for honest dissent on some of these issues. I can only try to open the doors a little to that dissent as I sense the people and officials are ready to listen.

It has been a long journey for me to arrive at the peace that is now mine. Many men come out to themselves and to others much earlier in life. At whatever age, however, this process has elements of fear, especially for priests or seminarians called to function publicly in a church that is not supportive. In order to help other homosexual priests or religious in this process, I offer the following suggestions.

Search out the reality of your sexual identity and own it. The very first principle of the spiritual life is to love yourself as God has created you. For years I was into denial of my true sexual identity because I was under the impression that homosexuality was a sickness, a disease of the mind, and arrested psychosexual development, a perversion, and ultimately a sinful orientation that a person willed to have. I was trying to deny all areas and expressions of that orientation. It doesn't work. It's not supposed to work! Marc Oraison, a leading French priest, doctor, and psychiatrist, had counseled homosexuals for over twenty-five years when he wrote that homosexuality is a given that no individual chooses. Criticism of a person for having such tendencies is therefore unjust because our sexual orientation is a fact that we each have to adjust to in our own way.[3] Trying to avoid this issue, I have found, only causes anger, compulsive behavior, hyperactivity, perfectionism, and then depression. Life will not be what you want it to be. I didn't create this; God did.

It might not be easy to admit, but this I believe is what Jesus was talking about when he said, "Blessed are the poor in spirit for theirs is the kingdom of God" (Matthew 5:3). I have talked to a number of priests who said the greatest moment of their lives was when they "came out" to themselves. When I first heard them say this, my reaction was that they were crazy. Now I realize that they were right, and even I can thank the Lord that I too have this gift to be used.

Build yourself a network of support. We all know how important, indeed necessary, positive role models and heroes are in our human development and growth. My own father was, for me, a model of patience, rugged individualism, and long-suffering. He was a very quiet person who worked by himself in his own business. He was a strong man both physically and ethically. His was hard manual labor, requiring top physical condition, which he maintained beyond retirement. His contracts with customers were verbal agreements that had the binding force of an American Indian bloodoath. He was a hero for me, a saint. But he wasn't gay.

With new awareness and understanding of myself as a gay man, I embarked on a search for gay saints and gay spirituality. By gay saints I envisioned people who saw their gayness as a blessing and a gift of the Spirit through, with, and in which God continues the building of his kingdom. The saints I found were not the people of past history who have been canonized by the church, but rather people of today, prophetic people who were risking career and active ministry to unveil a whole wealth of giftedness and spiritual treasures in those who find themselves homosexual. I was deeply impressed by the openness of these authors and their ability to identify the phobias, to articulate the issues involving the Scriptures and ethics, and to propose a spirituality for gay and lesbian Catholics.

For years specialists in aerodynamics wondered why Canadian geese fly only in the *V* formation. They discovered that each giant bird, while flapping its wings, creates an upward lift for the bird that follows. When all the geese do their part in a tight *V* formation, the whole flock acquires an amazing 70 percent greater flying range than if each bird flew alone. The specialists observed another phenomenon. When one bird begins to lag behind, the others "honk" him back into place.

What turned out to be an interesting discovery about animal life by engineers and scientists is simply a confirmation of a principle of life for all of us. I believe that my present emotional and spiritual health is a result of the support, love, affirmation, and "honking" from my network, which comprises a religious spiritual director (a woman), two clerical support groups (one specifically gay and the other not), a long-time married female friend and confidant, and the network already referred to called Communication Ministry, Inc.

It is generally recommended that every priest have a spiritual director. I think it is especially helpful for a gay priest. His sexuality makes him different from just about 90 percent of everyone else. His spiritual life must begin by considering this difference, not by ignoring it or by diminishing its importance. Indeed, one of the problems the gay priest faces in his spiritual life is precisely the pressure of the Church not to deal with the issue. "It is an anomaly. Shove it aside, and get on with living the Christian life," is the message we hear. However, since Vatican II there have developed spiritualities unique to diverse groups of people, including children, teenagers, young unmarried adults, the married, the divorced, the widowed, diocesan clergy, religious. These groups have specific needs and circumstances that form their spiritual journey. I believe the gay priest can also have his own.

I have asked my spiritual director to assist me in three areas of my life: to help identify what the Lord has done for me in my uniqueness and difference as a gay priest; to identify what gifts and pitfalls, strengths and weaknesses, grace and sin are operative in my life now that I have come out; and to identify the challenges, supports, obstacles, and resources to further my emotional and spiritual maturity.

I have also made a point of developing a deep and honest friendship. We get together for coffee or lunch every few weeks. We compare notes about our life experiences. She helps me to realize that it is not just gays or men who have challenges and changes to go through in their development. And as a woman, a mother, a grandmother, she views things from a different perspective and gives me balance. The fact that I am gay and she is a married woman also takes the sexual threat away from our relationship, releasing us from game playing.

My gay clergy support group meets once a month. There is time for prayer, for sharing what is going on in our lives. These types of support groups exist in different parts of the country. The gay groups might be harder to find because of the anonymity needed to protect participants from harassment. They are easy enough to start. If you know one other gay priest he probably knows one other, and quickly there can be a group. That at least is how we got started. The group should not grow larger than eight to ten members, so that everyone has the chance to speak. It is important to guarantee confidentiality as to both the membership and the content of the discussions. It is also important that the members make a commitment to be present regularly so that there is continuity and trust can grow.

Learn about the recent biblical scholarship regarding homosexuality. The Bible is an indispensable source of Catholic tradition and spirituality. We have to be grounded in the Scriptures. If the Scriptures are against us, who can be for us? A superficial reading of the sacred Word does seem to condemn homosexuality. This has been the cudgel to beat down the homosexual person and leave him or her spiritually bashed. However, an ever-increasing number of scriptural scholars are cautioning against a literalist and fundamentalist acceptance of Bible passages that appear to speak against the modern understanding of constitutional homosexuality. If we truly respect the Word of God we will take the time to learn what this Word really says and not simply what we think it is saying or want it to say. One can be certain that such studies, no matter what results are reached, will provoke heated opposition.

I believe that the freedom and objectivity of this emotionally charged discussion and the sense of responsibility with which it is conducted will be the real test of the maturity of modern Catholic biblical scholarship in our post-Vatican II church.

Search for the new data in the behavioral sciences. In the pastoral constitution of the Church in the modern world, the Second Vatican Council urges us to blend modern science and its theories with Christian morality and doctrine. This is why the letter of Cardinal Ratzinger on homosexuality was such a scandal for the Church. It ignored contemporary scientific data in its analysis. The only sources cited in his letter were previous Vatican documents. There were no scientific data at all.[4]

The best scientific studies are telling us that there is a great deal more to know before we can say the last word on homosexuality. No simple equation can be written to explain homosexual development. The best thing science can do is proceed slowly and carefully as it tries to dissipate the clouds of darkness that still shroud our full understanding. Nevertheless, the American Psychiatric Association removed homosexuality from its list of sexual deviations in 1973, and many recent studies are showing this orientation as normal for a certain percentage of the population. The reason so many gays are feeling good about being gay, are sensing new energy and well-being in their acceptance of being gay, is precisely because it is a good and healthy expression of one aspect of creation.

Pray and meditate out of the experience of your gayness. My gay life experience is part of my prayer life and, I think, that of any religious or layperson; if one is gay it is so much a part of who one is that it must be part of the prayer. The Lord is bringing us through these experiences to himself. I realize that my relationship with another man, while officially discouraged by the Church, is actually bringing me closer to the Lord. I see in that relationship not an opposition to the Lord but another reason to thank God and grow closer to him. It has helped me grow in intimacy with God.

I go further. In prayer I say, "Lord Jesus, you are the fullness of humanity. You are gay, and you are heterosexual. You know what it means to have a relationship with men and with women. You came to experience everything in our life except sin." So I asked the Lord to be my lover. And in my imagination, I take his hand, I wipe his brow, I hold him in my arms, I listen to his heartbeat. Shocking? Why does it seem so blasphemous to some to think of Jesus laughing or smiling, hugging or kissing a human being of the same sex? These are the things that loving human beings do.[5]

When I was an adolescent I was introduced to a method of prayer attributed to Saint Ignatius Loyola. It is a method of imagining Gospel sentences in such a way as to personally involve the one who is meditating in a dialogue with the Lord. I've used it a lot as I've reflected on my sexuality.

For example, in the Annunciation, could I hear the angel say to me, "You are full of grace"? Could I believe that? As a homosexual, how can I be full of grace? It is easier to hear, "You are full of evil." I used that for a prayer and began to feel a movement of the Lord saying, "Your homosexuality is not an evil, not a sin; it is a gift, a charism."

When I imagined Mary going to visit her cousin Elizabeth, I saw Mary wanting to help Elizabeth but also Elizabeth helping Mary. Mary was inexperienced. She needed the wisdom of the older woman. From this I saw the importance of my own networking, joining with others for help and support.

Another meditation on the finding of Jesus in the Temple brought me to a most interesting insight about my own journey of faith. I reflected on my search for Jesus, who seemed to be lost to me as I struggled to know my identity. It wasn't very joyful. And then I put myself into Jesus' position. Through his questions and discussions with the rabbis he must have realized early on that his mission could not fit into the traditional religious structure. He did not become a scribe, priest, rabbi, Pharisee, or Sadducee. He had to work outside the normal structures, but not outside the faith. It must have been very difficult for him. Indeed, it cost him his life. And even his parents did not understand. I sensed my own isolation insofar as I do not accept the normal parameters of Church teaching on my homosexuality. But I take comfort from Jesus that I can still work within the context of the faith.

Realize that in coming out you are not just dealing with a psychological problem but a question of social justice. The problems that you face are not caused by you personally but are the result of long-standing social oppression. Whatever personal insecurities and neurotic symptoms you might have, a good part of your lack of self-worth is because of what the heterosexual world around you is saying about you.

Our oppressive situation is an atmosphere, even a tradition, in which gay persons cannot and should not be proud of their identity; in which expression of that identity is a sin; and worst of all, in which that identity does not have a right to be acknowledged in any public way, in society and especially in the Church. It is an oppressive situation *par excellence* because it attacks what gay and lesbian persons *are*, not just what they do.

Our challenge is therefore even greater than that of the poor in Latin America. The poor in Latin America are visible, while we, 20 million in the USA, are for the most part invisible and paralyzed by fear. Is there a greater travesty of God's purposes than this? Does anyone see the mental torture that millions of gay people go through, especially the young? And can we ever begin to measure the ravaging effects upon the personality of years of fear, secrecy and socially induced guilt? This is the morass from which we must lift up our heads, and out of which we must rise.[6]

The National Conference of Catholic Bishops has said that homosexuals have a right to respect, friendship, and justice.[7] Coming out is not simply a personal odyssey; it is a social justice issue. It is part of the process of freeing a whole class of people. In order to help others overcome their fears, I must overcome mine. And to help them overcome their fears and the damage of prejudice is not optional. As the Synod of Bishops said in Rome in 1974:

Action on behalf of justice and full participation in the transformation of the world appear as constitutive dimensions of the preaching of the Gospel, or, in other words, of the Church's mission for the redemption of the human race and its liberation from every oppressive situation.[8]

My life as a parish priest involves so much more than the "gay issue." There are the daily priestly commitments to people: preparation and celebration of the sacraments; religious education for ages eight to eighty; visitation and pastoral care of the sick, dying, and housebound; ecumenical dialogue and fellowship; participation in neighborhood associations; administrative and managerial structures that require my presence and leadership at countless meetings. And there are also my regular priestly obligations toward the people in parish renewal, charismatic prayer groups, and Bible study.

But my "difference," my gayness, with all its fear, marginality, and ambiguity, has allowed me to identify all the more with the compassionate Jesus as I go about the building of his kingdom of love, justice, and peace. I have made mistakes in this area, and I must be ready to suffer the consequences. Overall, though, I rejoice and am glad.

Hanging on the wall of the rectory hallway is a plaque with a picture on it of Dr. Martin Luther King, Jr. Below his picture is the following quote:

If a man happens to be thirty-six years old, as I happen to be, and some great truth stands before the door of his life, some great opportunity to stand up for that which is right and that which is just, and he refuses to stand up because he wants to live a little longer and is afraid his home will get bombed, or he is afraid he will lose his job, or he is afraid he will get shot . . . he may go and live until he is eighty, and the cessation of breathing in his life is merely the belated announcement of an earlier death of the spirit.

Man dies when he refuses to stand up for that which is right. Man dies when he refuses to stand for that which is true. So we are going to stand up right here . . . letting the world know we are determined to be free.

Dr. King's words were like a personal letter to me. I was deeply moved. I felt the Lord's presence in the message. I knew it was time to make some decisions. A new birth was about to begin. I had to stand up and face my fears of being the least, the last, the lost, and the lonely. I hope you can, too.

5. Where Do We Go From Here?

REV. K. LAWRENCE

The purpose of this book is to initiate dialogue between gay Roman Catholic clergy, the Church, and the society around them. We have tried to make people aware that there is a large number of priests who are gay and that these priests have both special needs and special gifts to bring to ministry. However, there has been a major difficulty in bringing up the issue. The majority of gay priests, we believe, are not ready to "go public" because of the fears that have been discussed in earlier chapters. How does one conduct dialogue with a partner who feels he must remain silent, or at least anonymous? Two important questions, therefore, remain to be asked in this final chapter of the book: First, is the Church and the society ready to accept the reality of gay men in the clergy and to listen objectively to their experience? Second, is the moment opportune for gay clergy to publicly declare themselves and to speak out about their experience?

If the authors of this book did not believe that the answers to these questions were affirmative, they would not have bothered to write it. Yet, the affirmative answers are not without qualification.

One of the biggest problems for many people right now is the statement that was recently issued by the Congregation for the Doctrine of the Faith.[1] It states that "special concern and

---

Rev. K. Lawrence is the pseudonym of a gay priest.

pastoral attention should be directed toward those who have this condition [homosexuality], lest they be led to believe that the living out of this orientation in homosexual activity is a morally acceptable option. It is not" (par. 3). "Although the particular inclination of the homosexual person is not a sin, it is a more or less strong tendency ordered toward an intrinsic moral evil; and thus the inclination itself must be seen as an objective disorder" (par. 3). After laying out its arguments from Scripture, the document goes on to say that "to choose someone of the same sex for one's sexual activity is to annul the rich symbolism and meaning, not to mention the goals, of the Creator's sexual design. Homosexual activity is not a complementary union, able to transmit life" (par. 7). The document calls the homosexual orientation "essentially self-indulgent" and claims that "homosexual activity prevents one's own fulfillment and happiness by acting contrary to the creative wisdom of God" (par. 7). Although the letter affirms the homosexual person's "God-given dignity and worth," it cautions the bishops about many programs that may seek to pressure the Church to change its teaching, even while claiming not to do so (par. 14). "No authentic pastoral programme will include organizations in which homosexual persons associate with each other without clearly stating that homosexual activity is immoral," the document claims (par. 15). These are hardly statements meant to foster dialogue. Nevertheless, if we take one step back from the argument, there might be some reason for hope.

Both the Vatican and the gay liberation movement often seem to say that "gay" means principally genital behavior or the desire for it with members of one's own sex. That is a narrow view of what it means to be gay. The genital aspect of sexuality (genitality) is a part of a much broader phenomenon: Whom do we love and how? How do we bond with one another? How is a person's affective life organized, centered, focused? Being gay touches the very core of our being. It delineates and illuminates our characteristic way of coming to know ourselves and entering into relationships with others, our way of freeing up our energies so that they may produce life as they allow us to share love.

Straight people should rightly feel insulted by anything that defined their being in exclusively genital terms. The genitality itself is a vehicle for interaction, for bonding, for bringing about life and love, for self-definition in a way that underscores the fundamental drive for community and love that characterizes us as human beings. Being gay is simply another way of getting on with the task of growing to become clearer manifestations of God's love and life in our own world.

Gay priests themselves sometimes err in the identification of homosexuality with genitality because so many of them are late bloomers in terms of sexual identity issues. Often the principal stimulus that keeps pounding away at us until we have to acknowledge something going on in our lives is the stimulus of plain old sexual desire. Being sexually attracted enough to other men finally becomes something we cannot deny any more, no matter how hard we try. But so much of the integrative work of our personality formation is already accomplished, or at least relatively well along its way, that the process of integrating our sexuality into our personhood is more complex. We already have a sense of ourselves as persons, so the sexual side of us is just that dark area that we lived without for so long. We are trapped, as are so many other people, into confusing sexual identity and desire with genitality.

In the extreme this problem develops into an attitude I have frequently enough encountered among gay priests and seminarians: there is nothing wrong with genital activity, as long as it does not lead to a relationship! The relationship is what is perceived as threatening to priestly and religious life, not the satisfaction of the genital urges. This attitude reinforces both the identification of sexuality with genitality and the isolation of our sexuality from the rest of our lives. We priests often complain that people think of religious experience as only a Sunday phenomenon, but we often are guilty of the same thing with our sexuality. It is a late night, one-on-one, rest stop or gay bathhouse, or some other similarly partial manifestation of what should be central and integrative in our lives.

Perhaps the biggest problem for many people that came out of the Congregation for the Doctrine of the Faith's most recent statement on homosexuality is the assertion that homosexuality is an objective disorder because it is an inclination that would lead persons to commit intrinsically evil acts. This is a way of rephrasing the distinction between being homosexual (not sinful) and homosexual activity (sinful). This new distinction seems to be arguing specifically against the battle cry of the gay liberation movement, "Gay is good." The Vatican teachers reject this; for them gay is disorder.

The problem is that there are several different levels of thought going on here. "Gay is good" is an undifferentiated statement. It does not say what "gay" is, and it does not indicate what kinds of goodness are being attributed to it.

Let me use an analogy from the straight or heterosexual world. A rapist, a man in his twenties with a long line of sexual conquests notched on his belt, an occasional adulterer, a celibate priest, and a happily married and consistently faithful husband are all perhaps "straight." These examples, however, indicate that "Straight is good" is an abstraction of the highest order. The orientation may or may not be good as it is lived out in practice, depending on a wide variety of possibilities and circumstances. The rapist is obviously someone whose sexuality is not well integrated in his life. His affective development with regard to at least some women and himself is stunted or perverted. The possibility of love and mutual respect is replaced by hostility, fear, and conflict. "Straight is good" is far too general a statement, therefore, and so is "Gay is good."

The Vatican's response that gay is an objective disorder is no less obfuscating. If "Gay is good" is an abstraction, then so is "Homosexuality is an objective disorder" an abstraction. Actually, Catholic teaching has long insisted that human nature itself, affected by original sin, is objectively disordered. Left to our own unredeemed desires, we are inclined to sin. It is only when humanity is transformed through the action of grace that the orientation to sin is reversed. So of what help is it in the dialogue to use this term to apply specifically to homosexuality? Furthermore, to use the term *disordered* does not do justice to the rich textures and subtleties of humanity. It does not begin to investigate and discover how that humanity may be transformed in the Christian experience and lives of gay human beings.

"Gay is good," in the long run, I think, is trying to get at the reality that men can truly love men, and women love women, in a human and holistic way. However, it would be very good if we could all get rid of our slogans long enough to begin to do justice to the complexity of our humanity. "Gay is human" might say more than "Gay is good" or "Gay is a disorientation." It at least states a more basic claim and allows a starting point for dialogue.

It is critically important for us to be realistic in our expectations of any dialogue, however. We are not going to solve the problem of being gay priests in our generation, even though it is already true that for many of us being gay priests is less a problem and more a gift. We are not going to convert the pope and the hierarchy. After all, they too are men who are graced, but men who have to deal with their own issues.

I have known many gay priests and religious who, off and on for fifteen years, have been watching the evening news and waiting for the *National Catholic Reporter* to tell us that we have finally been approved, validated, and appreciated by those in authority. Their own lives have been in a kind of holding pattern until the "controllers" instruct them to change direction. They long to hear things like, "It's okay to be gay, even good to be gay, and here is what it means and what is now permissible for priests who share this curse-become-blessing." They think, "Surely the Church [read, hierarchy] will change the rules on celibacy once they understand us and approve us."

There is something peculiarly American in all this. If the rules or laws are against us, then all we have to do is change the laws and we will be officially okay. Maybe, but that is not the way it has worked for blacks or women. As deep-seated as the prejudice against them may be, few groups are nonetheless as unsettling to the males in control of "civilization," even in the Church, than men who love other men and dare on top of that to want to go on ministering as priests.

My point here is simple. Putting our lives on hold until things change is going to keep us deeply frustrated. If we wait for approval before we can feel affirmed enough ourselves to radically affirm and challenge others, we will probably die waiting. We need to grow up and get on with our lives. The ministry of service that is the substance of authority in the Church is not made any more clear or effective if we join the long lines of those who are eager to hand over responsibility for central areas of their own lives.

This brings us to our second question: Should gay priests publicly "come out"? There is no categorical answer, for there is no one way of being a gay priest, any more than there is one way of being a gay human being or a human being at all. We have taken, and we will continue to take, different paths to wholesomeness as our God continues to lead us and to push us through the circumstances of our individual and collective lives. It is essential, though, that we be able to make choices for ourselves to be the gay priests we are called to be. It is equally important in this context to remind ourselves that the life of each of us is a gradual process and that none of us, hopefully, will become stagnated or fixated at one particular stage of our own growth. Just as psychological or spiritual growth is not inevitable, so its meandering through the years is not inevitably clear or predictable.

Most priests, for reasons already discussed in this book, will choose to "come out" only to a small coterie of friends, if they come out to anyone at all. Many continue to deny their sexuality to themselves. Being aware of this fact, I intend to make some remarks in favor of those relatively few who will choose to be more open about their human orientation as gay.

To insist that being gay is some awful penalty, some curse, some disorder is a sign of great injustice or at the very least a sign of great ignorance. Indirectly, it is a means of exercising control over the identity of others. To call someone sick or depraved or objectively disordered (as seems to be intended by the Vatican) is patronizing and debilitating. It is also a sign of blindness, an unwillingness to confront the existence of people who seem to be different. It puts artificial limits on the human potential to realize God's loving and life-giving presence and power in our midst. Therefore, it cannot be ignored. Justice demands a response.

As a gay priest, however, I am not particularly interested in attacking Church leaders or anyone else for the ways in which they have oppressed us and continue to do so. Paranoia, after all, even the belligerent type, is hardly an adequate or worthwhile form of self-defense—nor does it stimulate growth. In addition, after all, we are all guilty of oppressing other people, whether the poor, women, blacks, the unattractive, or anyone else. And in some senses worse still, we oppress ourselves and one another precisely as gay. Most of us have so internalized the value system of those who dominate our culture and our church that we let our own freedom and our own power die on the vine. We tolerate pockets of self-hatred where there should be a healthy self-love that enables us to enter into truly loving and life-giving relationships. I'm not talking here about one-on-one relationships that have a genital component, principally because I don't believe that kind of relationship is the only or the most significant kind of relationship of which we are capable. I'm talking more about relationships of friendship, ministry, community life, and other forms of human interaction that witness to the grandeur and scope of human possibilities.

To some extent, the victims of oppression always must cooperate in their own oppression if it is going to continue. This is a complex phenomenon, and not one that I will spend a great deal of time discussing here. Perhaps some examples in our own context will make the point more clear. If I live in constant fear of being discovered to be a gay priest, I am accepting my own diminishment and cooperating in my subjugation. If I feel I have to act "super macho" to prove I'm a man or tell "fag" jokes to throw other people off the scent, or cultivate cover relations with women to convince them (and myself?) that I'm really "normal," I'm voluntarily diminishing my own freedom and self-worth. If I accept the rationale of my bishop or provincial that it's OK to be gay, but, for God's sake, keep it to yourself so you don't give scandal or confuse people—as though our official positions didn't give scandal often enough themselves and people weren't already confused!—I am not just accepting my own diminishment. By allowing other people's fears and prejudices to so control me that I'm always schizophrenic, thinking one thing and acting another, I am also accepting the diminishment of my own identity, so central to defining who I am and enabling me to enter into healthy and loving relationships. I am accepting restrictions on my ministry of proclaiming the good news of Jesus Christ. We have to take a long, hard look at the fact that the God we serve and embody has been consistently rejected—crucified in his own life among us—and that we should be very circumspect about expecting much different in our own lives.

In this sense, the current American (even ecclesial) preoccupation with self-fulfillment and growth has to be rejected when it is nothing more than a gradual slide into complacency. To feel radically good about ourselves is not to guarantee that we will "feel good." Radical self-acceptance is freeing and empowering—but it doesn't free and empower us to accept the standards of a society, some of whose members are bent on the final comfort, it frees and empowers us to be signs of contradiction, if need be, of a love so powerful that it can bring life out of death. When we celebrate as priests the memorial of Christ's death and resurrection, we ought to remind ourselves that the Christian way leads to life wrought out of death through the power of love. Being countercultural for gay priests may mean on some very profound level not accepting the crippling definition of ourselves that our Church, our society, and oftentimes we ourselves hand out.

If we assume that gay priests are fundamentally called to celibacy (which is admittedly arguable), and if we further assume (as previous chapters indicate) that being gay is truly a gracious gift from God, one that has the potential to enhance our ministry even as it deepens our own sense of identity and capacity to reach out to others—if we make these assumptions, then it seems clear that publicly acknowledged homosexuality among priests, some priests, could go a long way toward demythologizing homosexuality and showing it to be the potentially graced reality it often is. All the positive arguments in favor of coming out apply to priests—and some arguments apply specifically to priests.

Anyone who comes out runs the risk of persecution, oppression, misunderstanding, name-calling, and so on. And anyone who comes out knows the danger of his homosexuality's becoming the issue he has to keep dealing with endlessly. Some priests, however, it seems to me, are ideally suited to undergo these trials. They claim to be followers of Jesus Christ, who was himself persecuted. They don't have families who might be endangered by negative attitudes (I do not underestimate parents, brothers and sisters, etc.—I mean only that they won't have spouses or children subject to ridicule or worse). If they are celibate, they won't have to be particularly concerned about the implications of scandal involved in establishing relationships that are genitally oriented. If they are not celibate, presumably they will keep that to themselves and run no more risk of scandal and complication than the typical heterosexual but not celibate priest. (That course may, in fact, entail a fair amount of difficulty, but that hasn't stopped us from wanting the faithful to assume we're all healthy, red-blooded heterosexual males.)

In short, who has a greater chance or opportunity to put homosexuality into a broader context, explore the potential of its meaning, expose the empty abstractions or misconstrued "explanations" of it than a priest? Who has, or should have, more freedom to encounter painful possibilities—and the spiritual and emotional resources required to see that pain transformed into life-giving and redemptive love that expresses itself in significant service?

Unfortunately, it is common for priests to sublimate their sexuality, including the always more problematic homosexuality, in a pursuit of power and authority over others. The very heart of Christian authority and power, a radical form of openness and loving service, is perverted by a self-serving arrogation of control over others that reflects a fundamental lack of control over oneself. Ceding to others the power to control our understanding and expression of our own sexuality (not necessarily genitally, as I have indicated) can set us up all the more readily to buy into visions of power that have much more in common with a worldly evaluation of power, in the worst sense of the term, than with the power of God's grace, which brings life out of death and strength out of weakness.

A further service that can be performed by priests who come out lies in providing role models for other priests, seminarians, and religious. When I reflect that, more than twenty years ago when I was coming to terms with my own gayness in the context of a call to priesthood, there was no one who had gone before me to show me the way or ways to do this, when I reflect further that we are still often immersed in patterns of training and formation that continue to provide little or no concrete help to "our own" in this matter, that most gay priests and seminarians and religious have to reinvent the wheel when they confront issues of homosexuality and affectivity, I sense again the wonderful service that can be provided by those who feel called to be open about the reality of their homosexual identity. (Obviously, there are priests who have come out on many different levels already and who have made quite a contribution to us, their brothers; I am speaking of a broader phenomenon here.)

I continue to encounter seminarians and priests who feel compelled to learn about their sexuality in gay bars, for example, because they would never trust their rectors or spiritual directors or even their classmates to be able to accept them or help them. Even more, they fear precisely that their rectors will throw them out, their spiritual directors violate confidentiality and report them to superiors, and their class-mates either join in the process of turning them in or engage in "illicit" experimentation with them. The continued repression or denial of homosexuality as a simple and potentially graced way of life and ministry aggravates many problems that do not need to exist. Many of our "wounded healers" are a lot more wounded than they have to be simply because healthy role models are missing in their lives and in their training.

Granting all the real and potential horrors that face the gay priest who is openly gay, it is still a vivid sign of the Church's own weakness, sinfulness, and lack of courageous fidelity to its own mission that precisely those who, through an example of committed and dedicated and gay loving ministry, could do so much to witness in our troubled world to the richness of God's love are often constrained to fear greater persecution in the Church itself than outside it.

Let me again make clear that I have little interest in blaming the Church—we are all in the same boat, and we are all, after all, the same Church. I would not want to jeopardize or obscure the fundamental simplicity of my point here by resorting to futile expressions of anger and impotence that will get us nowhere. My point is simply that a healthy witness of homosexual priests could provide a wonderful service to others, and specifically to other priests, so that they may grow in an appreciation of their identity and of their gifts and not be mired throughout their lives in the felt need to dwell more on their sexuality (including its genital manifestations) than is either necessary or worthwhile. The very fact that homosexuality in the priesthood is still so much in the closet does not mean it goes away or is resolved or becomes unproblematic—quite the reverse can legitimately be hypothesized. To paraphrase Chesterton's celebrated remark about Christianity itself, we can't be sure that more openness about gayness in priests would not do a world of good—it has certainly never been tried!

Precisely because gayness has not been valued, treasured, and nurtured within the Church and its ministers, those ministers (like everyone else) have been forced to learn about their gayness and try to understand it and articulate it in often much less healthy environments and contexts. This is another variation of the Catch 22 theme. People (in the Church and outside it) decry the licentiousness and promiscuity of gay men—they go to these awful places and do abominable things with numerous other people! Yet it is equally true that, if gay men were accepted and understood and valued as human beings, there would be many more options available for them to meet and interact outside of "those awful places."

Many years ago, when I myself was in a bar-going phase of my life, the single most attractive element of going out was the sense of community and belonging I experienced in gay bars that I did not find in religious communities or seminary settings. I knew, quite simply, that for better or worse these people were by and large like me in at least one very important dimension. Since virtually no one in my religious setting was helping me feel anything but bad about myself as a sexual human being, I was powerfully impressed by the fact that these men took me as I was and made no big issue out of the fact that I was gay. I learned much about self-acceptance and honesty and integrity and dignity in settings that most people would still find to be offensive. In this context it is important to say a few words about AIDS.

We, gay priests, have begun to lie sick, to waste, and to die from AIDS. Priest friends of mine—up to now in relatively small numbers—have suffered this painful and tragic disease and have died. And some of them have died prematurely because they were so afraid of giving scandal or of being "uncovered" that they refused to risk medical treatment or hospitalization in their home cities. And if the statisticians and health-care people are to be believed, we have just witnessed the tip of the iceberg of AIDS and its ravages thus far—many more priests will succumb to it. And perhaps, at this point, the Church—all of us in the Church—can pause and ask ourselves, not why these priests were so bad (the ones who contracted it through sexual activity), but why we couldn't have made it easier for them to come to terms with their sexuality. Why have we frittered away vital energies in supporting and encouraging denial in our priests? Why have we rewarded at times with power and authority those men who have been afraid or unwilling to develop as affective and sexual human beings? Why have we offered so little help to "our own" that we may be on the verge of witnessing yet another decimation of our ranks, this time in those who fall sick and die long before their priestly ministry should have had to end by most standards?

One of the Church's proudest affirmations throughout the centuries has been that the blood of martyrs is the seed of Christians. Will God so bless us in the sickness and death of our priests that their death will not be in vain? Is it possible that we can avail ourselves of this opportunity to reflect that gay priests truly can and should be a leaven in our midst? Will we welcome the homosexuality of so many of our seminarians and priests as a precious ministerial treasure to be nurtured and cultivated? Can the deaths of this generation's priests from AIDS make it possible that future generations will not have to continue to work out their sexuality unassisted? Can the invisible gifts become more visible as we suffer in the crucible of this waste? In short, can we let our God work his mysterious way of bringing life out of death so that life and love may abound? This is a question we shall have to face. Make no mistake about it, we have begun to die, and it will be up to us, with the help of

God's grace, to see the redemptive possibilities of our suffering and death and discover and share some fragile human and Christian meaning with one another and with our world.

The early signs of "the world's" reaction to AIDS are far from heartening. Hysteria, victim-blaming, the closing of borders, retribution on our children, threats of mandatory testing, smug religious righteousness—we have seen all of this and will probably see more. The challenge to us in the Church cannot be more clear. Who will be the agents of God's love and compassion; who will help people see that there are deeper roots to this phenomenon than certain sexual practices; who will preach and believe that death can bring forth life in faith—who, if not us?

Contrary to what may appear to be the emotional tone of my previous remarks, I would like to state clearly and unequivocally that my predominant feeling about being a gay priest in today's Church and world is one of hope. I believe that the Eucharist is at the heart of any priestly sense of self-identity in service of our community. And I believe that the great action of prayer and of thanksgiving that we are privileged to celebrate is the most remarkable and unshakable foundation of any realistic hope. We believe that evil can be overcome—even our own evil. We give thanks for the death of a Son who is raised up from the dead through the unrelenting and unquenchable power of love. We believe that our God walks with us in our joys and hopes and legitimate triumphs—and that neither side of this equation that indicates the course of human life is complete without the other. We may see, in faith, as through a glass, darkly—but we see. Our lives are illuminated by the light of Christ that shines brightly in the darkness. We are priestly people, and a people of hope, because we believe that our high priest has wrought our salvation at the cost of his own life, a life that triumphs over death and bitterness and division because it is a life that is inseparable from love. As priests, and as gay priests, we are called to enter into that death in order to be agents of that life and of that love. This will be painful, but can we have any more realistic and firm ground for being men of hope?

Our ways of being gay and of being priests are and will be diverse. I personally have no illusions that, if we can only organize ourselves politically, shrewdly and strongly enough, we can overcome all resistance and sweep the Church and its leaders (and everyone else) along with us in a triumphant affirmation of our gifts and our gayness. I believe we can and have and will do a lot to break down resistance, and ignorance, and misunderstanding, and oppression. But we will do it in many different ways, if we remain faithful to our God and our own gifts. Some of us will come out, to a greater or a lesser extent. And we will pay the price, suffering our losses and savoring our successes. Most of us won't, and we will pay our own price, have our own losses and successes. As long as we— like everyone else—are free, we will be sinners in constant need of redemption. Let us at least support one another in the wondrous calling we have all received to be ministers of a life and a love that are stronger than death. Let us respect and care for ourselves, allowing our anger and frustration and pain to be transformed through the searing and purifying power of God's love into creative and constructive ways of being gay priests who treasure our gifts and share them with our communities. We do not have to accomplish everything to be able to accomplish something. Never before in the Church's history has there been such a potential to unleash and channel our gay energies as a leaven leading to as yet unknown upbuilding of the Body of Christ. May the God whose priest we are—happily and sadly, enthusiastically and with resistance, unworthily yet undeniably—bless us and all his people.

The title of this chapter is "Where Do We Go from Here?" We have tried in each chapter to begin a dialogue, to get some information out into the open. I have tried in this final chapter to suggest that basically we should continue in the direction we have set out on. Many of my own statements could be developed at much greater length and in much more detail.

Many of you, our readers, will no doubt disagree with much that has been said. We welcome that! Agree. Disagree. Clarify. Improve! Do all those good things and more, and our efforts will have been worthwhile. We have been keeping our light under a bushel basket; join us in the laborious process of dialogue and interchange that, with God's grace, will let the light shine out.

Appendix

Methodological Concerns

This project actually began when a small group of gay priests, most of the authors of the chapters in part II, decided that a collection of articles on the situation of the gay priest was needed. Since there appeared to be no scientific studies up to that time on sexuality and the priesthood (we were unaware of Wagner's research), it was decided that a random survey of all priests directly addressing issues of concern for both heterosexuals and homosexuals alike would be a productive start. Funds were solicited from private individuals to support the study, and Jim Wolf was contacted to coordinate the implementation of the survey and prepare an analysis of the results.

The first phase of the project was to develop a questionnaire that would not only provide information related to the various topics relevant to the book (i.e., sexuality, spirituality, attitudes toward preparation for the priesthood, and feelings about one's quality of life) but would also be an instrument that was applicable to any priest regardless of sexual orientation.

Since the intent of the survey was to use a simple probability sample of all priests in the United States to explore the relationship of sexuality to the lives of priests in general, a sample of one hundred priests was chosen from the *Official Catholic Directory* for the pilot test. Each potential respondent was sent a two-page cover letter explaining the purpose of the study along with a stamped return envelope, the questionnaire, and a letter from the chairman of the University of Chicago Department of Sociology verifying the author's status as a graduate student in good standing and that the department was aware of the research.

After an initial mailing in September, followed up by an additional mailing to all 100 in October, produced only 31 responses, it was determined that the planned random sample of 2,500 would most likely produce a sample of only about 775, with little hope of knowing how biased the results would be. Though a response rate of 31 percent to a mailed questionnaire might seem acceptable under most circumstances, we had every reason to believe that nonresponse was directly related to the subject under study. The random sample method was therefore abandoned.

While the pilot test was being conducted, an additional survey using a "snowball sample" technique was under way to contact only gay priests. Each of the priests involved in the project at the time received twenty copies of the questionnaire (reproduced in the following pages) and sent it to friends they knew were gay priests. We received requests from respondents for additional copies (sometimes ten or more) and ultimately ended up mailing out a total of approximately 250 questionnaires. Since only about 25 of the 101 responses we received appeared to be copies of our originals, it is assumed that the majority of the gay priests contacted, either by us or through one of the respondents, declined to participate for reasons discussed in chapter 1.

It is common in survey research to purposely oversample certain groups of people when those groups are expected to make up only a small proportion of the total responses. Done in a random manner, this type of oversampling allows for more reliable results and varieties of analysis when these sampling categories are properly controlled for during the analysis. In our case, the network sample of gay priests was nonrandom and intended primarily to be used only if the random sample of all priests proved unsuccessful, as it eventually did. For this reason, the data were not reliable enough to be used as the author's dissertation research, as is mentioned in the opening text of the questionnaire.

Numerous statistical tests of significance, based on the assumption of randomized sampling, are quite often inappropriately used on nonrandom samples. Even the now famous Kinsey report on male sexuality was the subject of a special investigation by the American Statistical Association.[1] Although the committee of methodologists was sympathetic to the data collection problems of Kinsey and his colleagues, they were highly critical of many "boldly stated" conclusions that appeared to be based more on speculation than on anything found in the data itself. More recent studies of marital and sexual behavior that have received wide coverage in the media could just as easily have been the subject of these remarks. Great care has been taken in the preparation of this report to avoid these problems associated with the kind of sample used while at the same time to gain as much information as possible from our survey results.

In addition to the specific questions we wanted to ask in our questionnaire, many items were taken from the NCCB survey of Catholic priests and from the questions used by Wagner in his interviews with gay priests. With the exception of the question on their future plans, these questions were asked in the first half of our questionnaire to avoid any possible bias from our more personal questions.

The decision was made during the construction of the questionnaire to allow for a wide variety of precoded answer categories. This included the modification of the possible answers to the questions taken from the NCCB survey. These additional answer categories were useful during the analysis of our data, but they did create some problems in comparing our results with those of the NCCB study. After careful consideration of how the analysis might be affected, the following recodes were made to our data. In view of the overall findings of our study, we felt that these necessary adjustments have no significant effect on the conclusions of this report. The variables that were recoded provide information that is important but merely supplimental to the conclusions and implications of our findings.

The first set of recodes were to the variables on sources of satisfaction (Table 3) and of problems (Table 4). The original questions, as they appeared in the NCCB survey, allowed four possible answers to each of the items listed. We provided a 5-point scale ranging from 0 ("Never") to 4 ("always"). The table below illustrates how the data from our survey was recoded into a 4-point scale:

| NCCB Categories | | Network Survey | |
| | | Original | Final |
Satisfaction	Problem	Values	Values
"Great Importance"	"A Great Problem"	3,4	3
"Some Importance"	"Somewhat of a Problem"	2	2
"Little Importance"	"Very Little Problem"	1	1
"No Importance"	"No Problem at All"	0	0

The problem of comparison was avoided in the discussion of the questions on spiritual experiences because substantial proportions from both surveys responded "never," an identical response on each questionnaire. The fact that nearly all the priests in each of the two studies responded something other than "never" to the sources of satisfaction and problems prevented a meaningful comparison of this response, thus necessitating recoding of our data.

The answer categories to the question on happiness (Table 6) was also different in the two studies. We allowed five possible answers; the NCCB study provided only three. Our data was recoded as follows:

NCCB Categories	Network Survey
"Very Happy"	"Very Happy"
"Happy"	"Happy, "Little of Both"
"Not Very Happy"	"Unhappy," "Very Unhappy"

Other wording differences are discussed in chapter 1.

Network Survey of Catholic Priests in the United States

Thank you for agreeing to participate in this study. By deciding to involve yourself in this research, you are contributing to a project which seeks to acquire information on the effects of sexuality on the lives of priests. At present there is much speculation, yet little information on how many priests, like yourself, consider themselves to be homosexual and whether or not this personal orientation has a significantly different effect on their lives as compared with the orientation of heterosexual priests. I am conducting this study for my dissertation research* and will be analyzing this information in conjunction with responses received from a national random sample of 2500 priests which is now in preparation. If you later receive a separate letter from me with an identical questionnaire, please take the time to fill that one out as well. This would mean that you have also fallen into the random sample for the country. Your participation in both is very important since the analysis of both the random sample and the network sample will be done separately yet will be of equal importance. However, please do not respond twice to either this form (labeled "Network Survey") or to the questionnaire mailed from me.

Before you begin answering any of these questions, please take the time to make at least one copy of this questionnaire. Most questions require that you circle a number which corresponds to an answer category; others are self-explanatory. Answer as many questions as you wish (preferably all) and mail your responses to me at the address found at the end of this form. Then contact as many priests as you wish who you know to be homosexual (celibate or active) and ask them if they would also like to participate in this study as you have. If so, please send them a copy of this questionnaire. Though some of the questions may seem a bit unrelated to the above mentioned goals, they are taken from previous surveys of priests and will aid comparability.

1) Please indicate the year you were: born 19__; first
   entered the seminary 19__; were ordained 19__.   [5–10]

2) Are you a: 0) Diocesan priest or 1) member of a religious order?   [11]

---

*Due to failure of random sample method, data was not used for author's dissertation.

3) How long have you been at your present
assignment? ____ year(s) [12–13]

4) Which of the following best describes your current
assignment?

-Type of assignment: (CIRCLE ALL THAT APPLY.) [14–22]
a) parish, b) teaching, c) monastic, d) student,
e) hospital, f) chaplain, g) counseling, h) administration, i) other.

-Location: (CIRCLE ONLY ONE.) [23]
0) Urban, 1) Suburban, 2) Rural.

5) What is the average age of most priests you know
well? CIRCLE ONE.

0) under 25, 1) 25–35, 3) 46–55, 4) over 55 [24]

6) What is the average age of the close friends you have
now? CIRCLE ONE.

0) under 25, 1) 25–35, 2) 36–45, 3) 46–55, 4) over 55 [25]

7) Are you generally happy or unhappy with your life?
CIRCLE ONE. [26]

0) very happy, 1) happy, 2) little of both, 3) unhappy, 4) very unhappy.

8) During the past two or three years, how often have
you experienced each of the following? CIRCLE ONE
NUMBER ON EACH LINE.

	NEVER			OFTEN		
a) An overwhelming feeling of being at one with God	0	1	2	3	4	[27]
b) A sense of being in the presence of God	0	1	2	3	4	[28]
c) A feeling of being afraid of God	0	1	2	3	4	[29]
d) A deep feeling of being personally loved by God here and now	0	1	2	3	4	[30]
e) A feeling of being tempted by the devil	0	1	2	3	4	[31]
f) A feeling of being abandoned by God	0	1	2	3	4	[32]
g) A spiritual force which lifted you out of your physical reality	0	1	2	3	4	[33]

9) How often are each of the following important sources of satisfaction for most priests you know well? CIRCLE ONE CODE ON EACH LINE.

	NEVER			ALWAYS		
a) Administering the sacraments	0	1	2	3	4	[34]
b) The respect received for being a priest	0	1	2	3	4	[35]
c) Administrative work of the Church	0	1	2	3	4	[36]
d) Intellectual and creative activities	0	1	2	3	4	[37]
e) Spiritual security of being a priest	0	1	2	3	4	[38]
f) Engaging in efforts of social reform	0	1	2	3	4	[39]
g) Working and developing friendships with others	0	1	2	3	4	[40]
h) Leading a celibate life	0	1	2	3	4	[41]
i) Hobbies (painting, cooking, etc.)	0	1	2	3	4	[42]

10) How often are each of the following important sources of satisfaction for you? CIRCLE ONE CODE ON EACH LINE.

	NEVER			ALWAYS		
a) Administering the sacraments	0	1	2	3	4	[43]
b) The respect received for being a priest	0	1	2	3	4	[44]
c) Administrative work of the Church	0	1	2	3	4	[45]
d) Intellectual and creative activities	0	1	2	3	4	[46]
e) Spiritual security of being a priest	0	1	2	3	4	[47]
f) Engaging in efforts of social reform	0	1	2	3	4	[48]
g) Working and developing friendships with others	0	1	2	3	4	[49]
h) Leading a celibate life	0	1	2	3	4	[50]
i) Hobbies (painting, cooking, etc.)	0	1	2	3	4	[51]

11) How often do each of the following pose problems to most priests you know well? CIRCLE ONE CODE ON EACH LINE.

	NEVER				ALWAYS	
a) The authority structure of the Church	0	1	2	3	4	[52]
b) Loneliness of priestly life	0	1	2	3	4	[53]
c) Leading a celibate life	0	1	2	3	4	[54]
d) Relations with superiors	0	1	2	3	4	[55]
e) Lack of chance for personal fulfillment	0	1	2	3	4	[56]
f) Relevance of the work priests do	0	1	2	3	4	[57]
g) Psychosexual development	0	1	2	3	4	[58]
h) Relevance of certain Church doctrine	0	1	2	3	4	[59]
i) Inability to develop close friendships	0	1	2	3	4	[60]

12) How often do each of the following pose problems for you? CIRCLE ONE CODE ON EACH LINE.

	NEVER				ALWAYS	
a) The authority structure of the Church	0	1	2	3	4	[1]
b) Loneliness of priestly life	0	1	2	3	4	[2]
c) Leading a celibate life	0	1	2	3	4	[3]
d) Relations with superiors	0	1	2	3	4	[4]
e) Lack of chance for personal fulfillment	0	1	2	3	4	[5]
f) Relevance of the work priests do	0	1	2	3	4	[6]
g) Psychosexual development	0	1	2	3	4	[7]
h) Relevance of certain Church doctrine	0	1	2	3	4	[8]
i) Inability to develop close friendships	0	1	2	3	4	[9]

13) Do you agree with this statement: "Homosexuality is a grave sin in the eyes of God"? CIRCLE ONE NUMBER ONLY.

Strongly agree. 0 1 2 3 4 5 6 Strongly disagree.   [10]

14) Do you agree with this statement: "Extra-marital sex is a grave sin in the eyes of God"? CIRCLE ONE NUMBER ONLY.

Strongly agree. 0 1 2 3 4 5 6 Strongly disagree.   [11]

15) How do you understand your commitment to celibacy? CIRCLE ALL THAT APPLY.

    a) It means total sexual abstinence as proof of my
devotion.   [12]

    b) It means forgoing marriage but not necessarily sex-
ual activity.   [13]

    c) It is an ideal rather than a law which must be
obeyed.   [14]

    d) It means attempting to avoid all acts of sexual
pleasure.   [15]

    e) I am uncertain at this time.   [16]

16) How easy is it for you to develop close friendships
with:

-women? (CIRCLE ONLY ONE.)   [17]
0) very easy, 1) easy, 2) so–so, 3) difficult, 4) very
difficult.

-men? (CIRCLE ONLY ONE.)   [18]
0) very easy, 1) easy, 2) so–so, 3) difficult, 4) very
difficult.

17) How would you describe your sexual attraction to:
-women? (CIRCLE ONLY ONE.)
Not at all attracted. 0 1 2 3 4 5 6 Very attracted.   [19]
-men? (CIRCLE ONLY ONE.)
Not at all attracted. 0 1 2 3 4 5 6 Very attracted.   [20]

18) How well would you say your seminary training has
prepared you to live the life of a priest? CIRCLE
ONLY ONE.   [21]
0) Very Well, 1) well, 2) so–so, 3) not very well, 4)
very badly.

19) Do you approve of encouraging young men to enter
seminary high schools? CIRCLE ONLY ONE.

0) Yes, 1) No, 2) Uncertain, 3) Other _____ [22]

20) Should others seek your advice on issues related to
sexuality, how would you most likely counsel:

-lay people? (CIRCLE ONLY ONE NUMBER.)   [23]
Follow your own conscience. 0 1 2 3 4 5 6 Follow
Church doctrine.

-other priests or religious? (CIRCLE ONLY ONE
NUMBER.)   [24]
Follow your own conscience. 0 1 2 3 4 5 6 Follow
Church doctrine.

21) How do you feel your life in the seminary influenced your sexual attitudes? (CIRCLE ONLY ONE NUM-BER.) [25]

Very positive influence. 0 1 2 3 4 5 6 Very negative influence.

22) Does being a priest enhance or inhibit your sexuality? CIRCLE ONE.

0) Enhances, 1) inhibits, 2) neither, 3) other _____ [26]

23) How would you rate your own sexual orientation? CIRCLE ONE. [27]

Completely heterosexual. 0 1 2 3 4 5 6 Completely homosexual.

24) At what age were you first aware of this orientation? _____ yrs. old.

25) Have you recently discussed concerns related to your own sexuality with any of the following people? CIRCLE ALL THAT APPLY.

a) Superior	b) Close female friend	[30–31]
c) Confessor	d) Therapist	[32–33]
e) Close male friend	f) Family member	[34–35]
g) Have not discussed this with anyone recently.		[36]

26) Which of the following best describes how you deal with celibacy? CIRCLE ONLY ONE. [37]

0) I abstain from sex with others because I feel I am forced to do so.
1) I abstain from sex with others because I choose to do so.
2) I consider my sexual life as separate from my life as a priest.
3) I have been unable to resolve this issue.
4) Other _____

27) Approximately what percent of Catholic priests in the U.S. do you think have a sexual orientation that is:

a) heterosexual? ____ %   b) homosexual? ____ %   [38–41]

28) Approximately what percent of Catholic seminarians in the U.S. do you think have a sexual orientation that is:

a) heterosexual? ____ %   b) homosexual? ____ %   [42–45]

29) How often do you feel that your attitudes regarding your own sexuality interfere with your work as a priest? CIRCLE ONLY ONE.

0) Never, 1) rarely, 2) occasionally, 3) often,
4) always   [46]

30) Prior to your ordination, how often were you sexually
active with other people? CIRCLE ONLY ONE.

0) Never, 1) rarely, 2) occasionally, 3) frequently.   [47]

31) How would you describe your sexual orientation prior
to your ordination? CIRCLE ONLY ONE.   [48]

0) Celibate heterosexual   1) Active heterosexual
2) Celibate homosexual   3) Active homosexual
4) Celibate bisexual   5) Active bisexual
6) Other (Please explain _____)

32) Since your ordination, how often were you sexually
active with other people? CIRCLE ONLY ONE.

0) Never, 1) rarely, 2) occasionally, 3) frequently.   [49]

33) How would you describe your sexual orientation since
your ordination? CIRCLE ONLY ONE.   [50]

0) Celibate heterosexual   1) Active heterosexual
2) Celibate homosexual   3) Active homosexual
4) Celibate bisexual   5) Active bisexual
6) Other (Please explain _____)

34) How involved have you been in the past with any
sort of human rights movement (either secular or
Church-related)? CIRCLE ONE ONLY.   [51]

0) I have been publicly active in such a movement.
1) I have supported such a movement in principle
but restricted my active involvement to discussions
with friends.
2) I have supported such a movement but rarely discuss my views on such matters with others.
3) I do not concern myself with such politically oriented issues.

35) If an organization existed within the Church to actively promote a more open dialogue between priests and
the hierarchy of the Church regarding issues of sexuality and the priesthood, how likely would you be to
get involved? CIRCLE ONLY ONE.   [52]

0) I would most likely become actively involved.
1) I would support such a movement, but I am not
certain I would become actively involved.
2) I am not certain I would support such a movement.
3) I would probably not support such a movement.

36) Which of the following statements most clearly reflects your current feelings about your future in the priesthood? CIRCLE ONLY ONE.   [53]
   0) I definitely will not leave the priesthood.
   1) I am fairly certain I will not leave the priesthood.
   2) I am uncertain about my future.
   3) I will probably leave.
   4) I have definitely decided to leave the priesthood.

37) [Optional] Please indicate the highest ranking position (or title) you have held in your career as a priest (Rev., Pastor, Abbot, etc.)   [54]

   _____. (Include more than one if necessary.)

38) Many personal questions have been asked of you in this survey. Please use the reverse side(s) of this questionnaire to add any additional comments you feel are necessary to clarify any of your responses as well as to suggest other ideas which have not been adequately addressed in this questionnaire.

Notes

FOREWORD

1. From the "Letter to the Bishops of the Catholic Church on the Pastoral Care of Homosexual Persons" dated October 1, 1986. During an audience granted by His Holiness, Pope John Paul II, this letter was approved and adopted in an ordinary session of the Congregation for the Doctrine of the Faith and ordered to be published over the name of Joseph Cardinal Ratzinger, prefect. It was made public at the Vatican on October 30, 1986.

CHAPTER ONE: HOMOSEXUALITY AND RELIGIOUS IDEOLOGY

1. H. McClosky, and A. Brill, *The Dimensions of Tolerance* (New York: Russell Sage Foundation, 1983), 199–207. J. A. Davis, and T. W. Smith, *General Social Surveys, 1972–1989* (machine-readable data file), principal investigator, James A. Davis; Senior Study Director, Tom W. Smith, NORC ed. (Chicago: National Opinion Research Center, 1989; Storrs, CT: The Roper Center for Public Opinion Research, University of Connecticut, distributor).
2. P. Ariès, and A. Bejin, eds., *Western Sexuality*, trans. by Anthony Forster (New York: Basil Blackwell, 1985).
3. R. Wagner, O. M. I., *Gay Catholic Priests: A Study of Cognitive and Affective Dissonance* (Ph.D. dissertation, Institute for Advanced Study of Human Sexuality; San Francisco, CA: Specific Press, 1981), 2–7.
4. For one of the most widely read critiques of the church's official interpretation of Scripture, see John Boswell's *Christianity, Social Tolerance and Homosexuality* (Chicago: Univ. of Chicago Press, 1980).
5. Augustine and Chrysostom, quoted in Wagner, *Gay Catholic Priests*, p. 4.
6. S. Bailey, "Homosexuality and Homosexualism," in *A Dictionary of Christian Ethics* (London: SCM Press, 1967), 152–153.
7. For the more cautious review, see C. Curran, *Catholic Moral Theology in Dialogue* (Notre Dame, IN: Fides Press, 1972). The more direct critique can be found in J. McNeill, S. J., *The Church and the Homosexual* (Kansas City, MO: Sheed Andrews & McMeel, 1976).
8. E. Rueda, *The Homosexual Network: Private Lives and Public Policy* (Old Greenwich, CT: Devin Adair, 1982).
9. Further evidence of the attitude that homosexuality is an illness is apparent in the interview with Colin Cook, director of the Quest Learning Center (C. Cook, and J. Spangler, "The 'H' Solution," in *Ministry* September 1981).

189

This center was instituted to help those who "wish to experience freedom from their homosexual identity."

10. Rueda, *Homosexual Network* , 299–370.

11. G. De Stefano, "Gay Under the Collar: The Hypocrisy of the Catholic Church," *The Advocate*, February 4, 1986, 43–48.

12. R. Bellah, R. Madsen, W. M. Sullivan, A. Swidler, and S. M. Tipton, *Habits of the Heart* (Berkeley: University of California Press, 1985).

13. J. D'Emilio, *Sexual Politics, Sexual Communities* (Chicago: Univ. of Chicago Press, 1983).

14. A. Kinsey, W. Pomeroy, and C. Martin, *Sexual Behavior in the Human Male* (Philadelphia: W. B. Saunders, 1948); M. Weinberg and C. Williams, *Male Homosexuals: Their Problems and Adaptations* (New York: Oxford Univ. Press, 1974); Wagner, *Gay Catholic Priests*; M. Ross, "Actual and Anticipated Societal Reaction to Homosexuality and Adjustment in Two Societies," *Journal of Sex Research* 21 (February 1985): 40–55.

15. For an extensive analysis of the NCCB data, including the information collected on priests who had resigned or retired, see A. Greeley and R. Schoenerr, *The Catholic Priest in the United States: Sociological Investigations* (Washington, DC: United States Catholic Conference, 1972).

16. E. Kennedy and V. Heckler, *The Catholic Priest in the United States: Psychological Investigations* (Washington, DC: United States Catholic Conference, 1972).

17. Emphasis added. Weinberg and Williams, *Male Homosexuals*, 363.

18. Uncited quotations are taken directly from the written comments we received from our respondents. Occasionally words or phrases are placed in brackets to indicate they are substitutes for more specific original language that might have jeopardized the anonymity of the respondent.

19. De Stefano, "Gay Under the Collar," 47.

20. Wagner, *Gay Catholic Priests*.

21. Wagner, *Gay Catholic Priests*.

22. J. DeCecco, ed., "Controversy over the Bisexual and Homosexual Identities: Commentaries and Reactions," *Journal of Homosexuality* 10 (Winter 1984):3–4.

23. We decided not to pursue specific enumeration of sexual activity because of the highly sensitive nature of the topic. Such information is best collected through personal interview techniques like those used by Wagner.

24. See C. Tripp, *The Homosexual Matrix* (New York: McGraw-Hill, 1975). See especially pp. 94–159 for his discussion of sexual encounter patterns.

25. Wagner, *Gay Catholic Priests*.

26. G. Simmel, "The Stranger," in *On Individuality and Social Forms*, ed. Donald N. Levine (Chicago: Univ. of Chicago Press, 1971).

27. G. Simmel, "Conflict," in *Conflict and the Web of Group Affiliations* (New York: Free Press, 1955).

28. Weinberg and Williams, *Male Homosexuals*.

29. Ross, "Societal Reaction to Homosexuality."

CHAPTER TWO: INVISIBLE GIFTS

1. James B. Nelson (*Embodiment: An Approach to Sexuality and Christian Theology* [Minneapolis: Augsburg Publishing House, 1978], 86) quoting Dan Sullivan. Also very helpful in understanding this kind of sexual activity is Patrick Carnes's book *The Sexual Addiction* (Minneapolis: Compcare Publications, 1984). Carnes, a psychologist, builds a very convincing case for understanding some kinds of sexual activity as actually addictive, much as drugs or alcohol can be. Stemming from what Carnes calls four powerful but erroneous "core beliefs" (I am basically an unworthy person; No one would love me as I am; My needs are never going to be met if I depend on others; Sex is my most important need), sexual addictions lead to compulsive harmful and even criminal sexual behavior that can be controlled, but not cured, by support groups and therapy. I would say that a significant amount of anonymous sexual activity among priests and religious is due to addiction of this kind.

2. John Boswell, "Rediscovering Gay History: Archetypes of Gay Love in Christian History" (London: Gay Christian Movement, CBM Box 6914, London WC1N 3XX, 1982), 16–19. This monograph, one of the Michael Harding Addresses sponsored by the GCM, flows from his massive scholarly work, *Christianity, Social Tolerance and Homosexuality*, in which he tries to show that "the inherent opposition people assume subsists between homosexuality and Christianity is simply nonexistent." The monograph expands on this theory by describing a "gay marriage ceremony" from the Greek church of the ninth or tenth century that he calls a "ceremony for the making of spiritual brotherhood"—which was not, as he emphasizes, spiritual in the sense of being nonsexual or nonromantic. He suggests that these ceremonies (which were very early celebrations of Christian romantic love) provide a basis for reevaluation of our understanding of the origins of prejudice against homosexuality.

3. Basil Pennington, O.C.S.O., "Vocation Discernment and the Homosexual," in R. Nugent, ed., *A Challenge to Love* (New York: Crossroad, 1984), 235–244.

4. C. G. Jung, *Collected Works*, trans. R. F. C. Hull (New York: Pantheon, 1959), vol. 9, part 1, pp. 86–87.

5. Matthew Fox, "The Spiritual Journey of the Homosexual . . . and Just About Everything Else," in Nugent, *A Challenge to Love*, 199. See also, in the same volume, "The Christian Body and Homosexual Maturing," by James Zullo and James Whitehead, pp. 20–37, especially p. 36: "If no biological offspring issue from gay and lesbian intimacy and commitment, religious and cultural gains do spring off, reminding us—as does our tradition of celibacy—that Christian fecundity is not restricted to biological fruitfulness."

CHAPTER THREE: A CHRISTIAN SPIRITUALITY

1. For a better understanding of the idiosyncratic nature of sexual object choice, see Robert J. Stoller, M.D., and Gilbert H. Herdt, Ph.D., "Theories

of Origins of Male Homosexuality: A Cross-cultural Look," *Arch. Gen. Psychiatry* 42 (April 1985): 399–404; Steve Duck and Dorothy Miell, "Mate Choice in Humans as an Interpersonal Process," in *Mate Choice*, ed. Patrick Bateson (London: Cambridge Univ. Press, 1983). See also the bibliography in Mark Cook and Robert McHenry, *Sexual Attraction* (Oxford: Pergamon Press, 1978); Alan Bell et al., *Sexual Preference* (Bloomington: Indiana Univ. Press, 1981); Kinsey et al., *Sexual Behavior in the Human Male*. Also see Morton Kelsey and Barbara Kelsey, *Sacrament of Sexuality* (Warwick, NY: Amith House, 1986), esp. chap. 9, "Homosexualities, Bisexualities, Psychology and Religion," pp. 180–208.

2. Erik Erickson, *Childhood and Society*, (New York: W. W. Norton, 1950), 263.
3. Gregory M. Herek, Ph.D., "Beyond 'Homophobia': A Social Psychological Perspective on Attitudes Toward Lesbians and Gay Men," Yale University, *Journal of Homosexuality* 10 (Fall 1984): 1.
4. For more information on body language, see Desmond Morris, *Manwatching: A Field Guide to Human Behavior* (New York: Harry N. Abrams, 1977); or Julius Fast, *Body Language* (New York: M. Evans and Company, 1970).

CHAPTER FOUR: THE FEARS OF A GAY PRIEST

1. A Statement by black bishops of the United States appeared in *Origins*, November 28, 1985.
2. Communication Ministry, Inc., P.O. Box 2272, Times Square Station, New York, NY 10108.
3. Marc Oraison, *The Homosexual Question*. Translated by Jane Zeni Flinn. (New York: Harper & Row, 1977).
4. J. Ratzinger, "Letter to the Bishops of the Catholic Church on the Pastoral Care of Homosexual Persons," *Origins*, November 13, 1986.
5. J. Ohanneson, *And They Felt No Shame: Christians Reclaiming Their Sexuality* (Minneapolis: Winston Press, 1983), 64–65.
6. *Communication*, Communication Ministry, Inc., June/July 1986.
7. National Conference of Catholic Bishops (NCCB), *To Live in Christ: A Pastoral Reflection on the Moral Life*, (Washington, DC: 1976), 19.
8. National Conference of Catholic Bishops (NCCB), "On Behalf of Voiceless Victims of Injustice: Human Rights and Reconciliation," in *Origins*, November 7, 1974.

CHAPTER FIVE: WHERE DO WE GO FROM HERE?

1. J. Ratzinger, "Letter to the Bishops of the Catholic Church on the Pastoral Care of Homosexual Persons," *Origins*, November 13, 1986.

APPENDIX

1. W. Cochran, F. Mosteller, and J. Tukey, *Statistical Problems of the Kinsey Report on Sexual Behavior in the Human Male* (Washington, DC: American Statistical Association, 1954). Although the review committee was sympathetic to the constraints Kinsey was working under, they were nonetheless critical of his tendency to overgeneralize his findings and use inappropriate methods of analysis for a nonrandom sample such as his.

Bibliography

Allport, G. W. *The Nature of Prejudice*. New York: Addison-Wesley, 1954.

> This comprehensive review of research in social psychology related to prejudice set standards for the discipline that remain unchallenged. Allport's lucid analysis provides timeless insight into the causes of prejudice and the implications of its manifestation in discrimination.

Archdiocesan Commission on Social Justice. *Homosexuality and Social Justice: The Report of the Task Force on Gay and Lesbian Issues of the Archdiocese of San Francisco*, 1982.

> The report was revised in 1986 and is available from The consultation on Homosexuality, Social Justice, and Roman Catholic Theology, 584 Castro Street, Room 341, San Francisco, CA 94114. This is the well-known report of the commission formed by the Archdiocese of San Francisco, which was disbanded shortly after the report was issued. Kevin Gordon, one of the members of the commission, immediately reconstituted the group as the Consultation of Homosexuality, Theology, and Social Justice, and the group, a think tank of lay theologians, psychologists, and other specialists, is now based in New York. The report contains sections on violence, family, language, spirituality, gay men and lesbians in religious life, and education, and contains a bibliography and policy recommendations in each area.

Ariès, P., and A. Bejin, eds. *Western Sexuality*. Translated by Anthony Forster. New York: Basil Blackwell, 1985.

Bailey, S. "Homosexuality and Homosexualism." In *A Dictionary of Christian Ethics*, pp. 152–153. London: SCM Press, 1967.

Baltimore Archdiocesan Gay/Lesbian Outreach. *Homosexuality: A Positive Catholic Perspective*. 2034 Park Avenue, Baltimore, MD 21217.

A sixty-page booklet whose chapters provide "a much needed positive context for lesbian/gay issues within the Catholic tradition." Written in a question and answer format, it covers such things as sexual ethics, parental questions, myths, teenage sexuality, biblical scholarship, and fundamentalist homophobia. A selective bibliography is included. Available for $2.00.

Bateson, P., ed. *Mate Choice*. London: Cambridge Univ. Press, 1983.

Bauman, Robert. *The Gentleman from Maryland*. New York: Arbor House, 1986. pp. 250 ff.

Bell, A., Ph.D., and M. Weinberg. *Homosexualities, A Study of Diversity Among Men and Women*. New York: Simon & Schuster, 1978.

Studies the wide diversity of life-styles and spiritualities within the homosexual world and gives accurate information about the social, religious, and political attitudes of gay people.

Bell, A., S. Hammersmtih, and M. Weinberg. *Sexual Preference*. Bloomington: Indiana Univ. Press, 1981.

Bellah, R., R. Madsen, W. M. Sullivan, A. Swidler, and S. M. Tipton. *Habits of the Heart*. Berkeley: Univ. of California Press, 1985.

Based on interviews with over two hundred Americans, Bellah and a team of researchers examine the contemporary role individualism plays in our sense of commitment to social institutions.

Black Bishops of the United States. "A Statement." *Origins* 15 (November 28, 1985): 395–399.

Boswell, J. *Christianity, Social Tolerance and Homosexuality*. Chicago: Univ. of Chicago Press, 1980.

Winner of the prestigious 1981 American Book Award for history, Boswell's book is perhaps most widely cited on the "official Catholic teaching" on homosexuality and its often-debated history by those hoping the Church will develop a more tolerant attitude. It is a revolutionary study of the history of attitudes toward homosexuality in the Christian West that helps elucidate the origins and operations of intolerance as a social force. "What will strike some readers as a partisan point of view is chiefly the absence of the negative attitudes on this subject ubiquitous in the modern West; after a long loud noise, a sudden silence may seem deafening" (p. xvi).

———. "Rediscovering Gay History: Archetypes of Gay Love in Christian History" (London: Gay Christian Movement, CBM Box 6914, London WC1N 3XX, 1982), pp. 16–19.

Brutchaell, J., C.S.C. "The Future of Our Fellowship: Transforming the Life of Vowed Communities." *Commonweal*, June 18, 1982, 364–370.

Though Burtchaell does not deal with homosexuality as such, he describes the changes he sees taking place in religious life as a result of changes in our understanding of priesthood and church: "Rank and status in the church and its ministries will no longer be the force sustaining our vowed memberships . . . what will emerge, when our monopoly [over the Church's work] is ended is that life in vowed communities properly [will have] as its *raison d'etre*, not certain ministries or even a privileged status in the Church's mission, but fidelity in the brotherhood or sisterhood as an alternative to marriage . . . our religious communities will emerge more clearly as our family, not our career" (367).

Bullough, V. L. *Sexual Variance*. Chicago: Univ. of Chicago Press, 1976.

A comprehensive overview of the historical and cross-cultural attitudes toward stigmatized sexual behavior in both Eastern and Western cultures.

Carnes, P. *The Sexual Addiction*. Minneapolis: Compcare Publications, 1984.

Cochran, W., F. Mosteller, and J. Tukey. *Statistical Problems of the Kinsey Report on Sexual Behavior in the Human Male*. Washington, D.C.: American Statistical Association, 1954.

This report is a sympathetic yet thorough examination of the problems associated with the classic "Kinsey Report." Though rarely discussed in the popular press, the methodology that Kinsey and his associates used had serious flaws that constrained their ability to generalize their findings.

Coleman, G., S.S., "The Homosexual Question in Priesthood and Religious Life." *Priest* 40 (December 1984): 12–19.

A reserved, but fairly tolerant appraisal of the possibility of accepting homosexual candidates for religious life and priesthood.

Communication Ministry, Inc. *Communications* 9:8 (June/July 1986).

Cook, C., and J. Spangler. "The 'H' Solution," in *Ministry*, September 1981.

Cook, M., and R. McHenry. *Sexual Attraction*. Oxford: Pergamon Press, 1978.

Curb, R., and N. Manahan. *Lesbian Nuns: Breaking Silence*. Tallahassee, FL: Naiad Press, 1985.

This collection of over fifty essays written by former and current nuns provides a fascinating look into the private lives of women who eventually learned they were lesbians, and into how that realization affected their lives as women devoted to Catholic religious communities. Two things are likely to impress the reader: how similar their experiences and the conclusions they reached were, and how many ended up rejecting the Catholic church as a legitimate religious institution.

Curran, C. *Catholic Moral Theology in Dialogue*. Notre Dame, IN: Fides Press, 1972.

———. "Moral Theology: Psychiatry and Homosexuality," in *Transition and Tradition in Moral Theology*, pp. 59–80. Notre Dame, IN: Notre Dame Press, 1979.

Curran develops a "theory of compromise" in light of modern psychiatry and awareness of the presence and effect of sin in Christian life. In this approach, he maintains "that the ideal meaning of sexual relationships is in terms of male and female . . . since heterosexual relationships are the ideal, all should strive in this direction." Still, "for an irreversible or constitutional homosexual, homosexual acts in the context of a loving relationship striving for permanency can be and are morally good" (71). Curran's position is midway between Church teaching and others who maintain that homosexual acts are purely good and natural. His "Moral Theology and Homosexuality," in *Critical Concerns in Moral Theology*, pp. 73–96 (Notre Dame, IN: Univ. of Notre Dame Press, 1984), is an updated version of this theory.

Daley, M., and M. Wilson. *Sex, Evolution and Behavior*. North Scituate, MA: Duxbury Press, 1978.

Davis, J. A., and T. W. Smith. *General Social Surveys, 1972–1989* (machine-readable data file). Principal investigator, James A. Davis; Senior Study Director, Tom W. Smith. NORC ed. Chicago: National Opinion Research Center, 1989; Storrs, CT: The Roper Center for Public Opinion Research, Univ. of Connecticut, distributor.

DeBlassie, R. "Affirming the Homosexual Priest." *Priest* 40 (April 1980): 34–36.

DeCecco, J., ed. "Homophobia: An Overview." *Journal of Homosexuality* 10 (Fall 1984): 1–2. Published under the same title by the Haworth Press, New York, 1984.

This volume represents the largest collection of articles on homophobia published to date. It includes theoretical analyses of the concept of homophobia, critiques and innovations pertaining to its assessment, its relationship to the biological sex of respondents, their perceived sex roles, and their etiological theories of homosexuality.

―――――. "Controversy Over the Bisexual and Homosexual Identities: Commentaries and Reactions." *Journal of Homosexuality* 10: (Winter 1984): 3–4.

DeCecco, J., and M. Shively, eds. *Bi-sexual and Homosexual Identities: Critical Theoretical Issues*. New York: The Haworth Press, 1984.

―――――. *Bi-sexual and Homosexual Identities: Critical Clinical Issues*. New York: The Haworth Press, 1984).

D'Emilio, J. *Sexual Politics, Sexual Communities*. Chicago: Univ. of Chicago Press, 1983.

This volume is one of the most frequently cited accounts of the emergence of the gay rights movement in America. D'Emilio traces the series of events, from subtle to explosive, that eventually brought the gay community onto the political scene as a viable force.

De Stefano, G. "Gay Under the Collar: The Hypocrisy of the Catholic Church." *The Advocate*, February 4, 1986.

Based in part on an interview with the psychologist and former Christian brother Kevin Gordon, as well as interviews with both active and former gay priests, this article examines the realities of gay clergy. Though one might expect the article to be biting and cynical, it is a fairly balanced and objective description of the experience of those interviewed.

Dignity Region V. *An Anthology for the Gay and Lesbian Community.* 3586 Whispering Brook Court, Grand Rapids, MI 49508, 1985.

Fast, J. *Body Language.* New York: M. Evans and Company, 1970.

Fortunato, J. E. *Embracing the Exile: Healing Journeys of Gay Christians.* New York: Seabury Press, 1983.

As a professional psychotherapist, the author writes about his faith journey through the psychological maze of homosexual awareness. Though at times a bit technical, he weaves the story of a powerful and successful struggle to embrace the exiled person within. He supplements the description and analysis of his own major life transitions with case histories of others.

Gallagher, J., ed. *Homosexuality and the Magisterium.* 4012 29th Street, Mt. Rainier, MD: New Ways Ministry, 1986.

A recent attempt to compile every magisterial statement that has appeared on homosexuality in the past decade. It includes a number of statements by individual bishops not readily available elsewhere.

Genovesi, Vincent, S.J. *In Pursuit of Love: Catholic Morality and Human Sexuality.* Wilmington, DE: Michael Glazier, 1987.

Genovesi's book is a cautious and sometimes wordy treatment of sexuality from a Catholic perspective, but it provides a good summary of recent literature as well as a helpful, progressive synthesis of its own. His conclusions are based largely on a proportionalist methodology.

Gill, J., S.J. "Homosexuality Today." *Human Development* 1 (Fall 1980): 16–25.

Gladue, B., Green, R. and R. Hellman. "Neuroendocrine Response to Estrogen and Sexual Orientation." *Science* 225 (September 18, 1984) : 1496–1499.

Grammick, Jeannine, and Pat Furey, eds. *The Vatican and Homosexuality: Reactions to the "Letter to the Bishops of the Catholic Church on the Pastoral Care of Homosexual Persons."* New York: Crossroad, 1988.

This is a collection of critical essays by writers from various disciplines. It presents a fairly good overview of the range of Catholic moral method and opinion.

Greeley, A., and R. Schoenerr. *The Catholic Priest in the United States: Sociological Investigations.* Washington, D.C.: United States Catholic Conference, 1972.

This report is an extensive analysis of a survey sponsored by the National Conference of Catholic Bishops in 1970. It was written in conjunction with the report published by Kennedy and Heckler (1972).

Guidon, Andre. *The Sexual Creators.* Lanham, MD: The University Press of America, 1986.

See especially chapters 7 and 8, "Gay Fecundity or Liberating Sexuality," and "Celibate Fecundity or Liberating Communities," which elaborate on Guidon's theory of sex as "language" that must be "spoken" ethically and his expansion of the traditional sexual norm of procreation to "fecundity," which is a broader understanding of generativity.

_____. "Homosexual Acts or Gay Speech?" In *The Vatican and Homosexuality: Reactions to the "Letter to the Bishops of the Catholic Church on the Pastoral Care of Homosexual Persons,"* pp. 208–215. Edited by Jeannine Grammick and Pat Furey. New York: Crossroad, 1988.

A briefer elaboration of the theory found in his earlier book *The Sexual Creators,* this essay is part of a diverse collection of responses to the Vatican's 1986 letter. Guidon argues that the expression "homosexual acts" should be dropped and sexual activity understood as *language,* because "when sexual activity is not animal but human, it does more than 'produce' things such as sensorial reaction, heat tumescence, orgasm, ejaculation or insemination. Human sex expresses and communicates emotions and meanings." Guidon's work is some of the most original in Catholic sexual morality.

_____. "Sexual Acts or Sexual Lifestyles: A Methodological Problem in Sexual Ethics." *Eglise at Theologie* 18(1987): 315–340.

A further refinement of Guidon's basic theory, which is critical of what he sees as the prevalent "act-centered morality" in the Roman Catholic approach.

Harvey, J., O.S.F.S. "Courage Encourages Gays." *National Catholic Reporter* 21 (January 18, 1985): 11.

John Harvey, founder of Courage, a support group for gays that moves toward celibacy, answers criticisms that he considers homosexuality a sickness and homosexuals to be self-hating and crippled. Robert Nugent presents an alternative view on the opposite page.

————. "An In-depth Review of Homosexuality: A New Christian Ethic." *Linacre Quarterly* 51 (November 1984): 341–349.

Helldorfer, M., F.S.C. "Genital Relationships: A Question of Integrity." In *Sexuality and Brotherhood*. Edited by Martin Helldorfer. Lockport, IL: Christian Brothers Conference, 1977.

He distinguishes "movements in the love experience" (caring/building a shared world/physical intimacy) and says that for the brother who falls in love, the question is inevitably, "We must move tenderness toward one another and away from the brothers, or we must tend toward the brothers and thus choose not to express our love genitally. It is a question of integrity: not to move in one direction or the other is to destroy the love relationship." He concludes that because of what happens to the act, the relationship, and the persons, "It is necessary to refrain from intimate sexual relations with a loved one if we choose to remain a brother" (p. 60).

Heston, L., M.D., and J. Shields. "Homosexuality in Twins." *Arch. Gen. Psychiatry* 10 (February 1968): 149–160.

Horner, T. *Jonathan Loved David: Homosexuality in Biblical Times*. Philadelphia: The Westminster Press, 1978.

This is a concise, reverent, and scholarly consideration of the biblical passages (Old and New Testaments) generally cited in connection with condemnation of homosexuality. Using available knowledge of both biblical languages and biblical cultures, Horner presents a balanced, consistent, and scriptually based acceptance of homosexuality in the context of a loving and life-giving relationship.

Jung, C. G. *Collected Works*. Translated by R. F. C. Hull. New York: Pantheon, 1959. Vol. 9, part 1, pp. 86–87.

Kelsey, M., and B. Kelsey. *Sacrament and Sexuality*. Warwick, NY: Amith House, 1986.

Kennedy, E., and V. Heckler. *The Catholic Priest in the United States: Psychological Investigations*. Washington, D.C.: United States Catholic Conference, 1972.

This report is the final analysis of a study sponsored by the National Conference of Catholic Bishops conducted in 1970. It coincided with the report published by Greeley (1972).

Kinsey, A., W. Pomeroy, and C. Martin *Sexual Behavior in the Human Male*. Philadelphia: W. B. Saunders, 1948.

————. *Sexual Behavior in the Human Female*. Philadelphia: W. B. Saunders, 1953.

Kraft, W. "Homosexuality and Religious Life." *Religious* 40 (May–June 1981): 370–381.

A fairly skeptical evaluation of the legitimacy of gay religious.

Kropinak, M. "Homosexuality and Religious Life." In *A Challenge to Love*, edited by Robert Nugent. New York: Crossroad, 1981.

Similar in thrust to B. Pennington's article (1984), but from a more specifically psychological and empirical standpoint, this article tries to show "that the homosexual person can be a mentally healthy person, that this person can live a lifestyle no less stable than that of a heterosexual person, and that there is no reason to exclude the homosexual person from religious life" (p. 245).

McClosky, H., and A. Brill. *The Dimensions of Tolerance*. New York: Russell Sage Foundation, 1983.

McClosky and Brill examine a variety of survey data in order to examine public attitudes related to civil liberty and expectations for conformity.

McNaught, B. *A Disturbed Peace: Selected Writings of an Irish Catholic Homosexual*. Washington, D.C.: Dignity Publications, 1981.

An honest, insightful personal description of the author's "fears, dreams, frustrations and joys" as a Catholic gay person. Says McNaught, who was fired from his job as a journalist for a Catholic newspaper: "I like being gay . . . [but] without the blessing of Church and society, my life is one outrageous experiment after another."

McNeill, J., S.J., *The Church and the Homosexual.* Kansas City, MO: Sheed Andrews & McMeel, 1976.

This book, which earned its author notoriety and a silencing from his superiors, was the first important book-length treatment of the topic and provides a valuable overview of the scriptural and theological questions. The controversy this book raised (evidenced by the withdrawal of the "imprimatur" for its second printing) underscores its very sensitive theme. It makes one of the more compelling arguments for the acceptance of "ethically responsible homosexual relationships."

Malloy, E., C.S.C. *Homosexuality and the Christian Way of Life.* Washington, D.C.: University Press of America, 1981.

Malloy finds the "homosexual way of life" to be basically incompatible with Christian values because of its "liberation conviction," which is deeply antithetical to the kinds of restraints and controls on sexual activity that Christian tradition upholds in the virtue of chastity. I agree with Charles Curran's criticism of Malloy's position ("Moral Theology and Homosexuality"), primarily its tendency to overgeneralize: Malloy does not demonstrate that homosexuals generally accept this "liberation conviction," nor that such liberation is necessarily opposed to Christian chastity.

Marmor, J., M.D. "Homosexuality: Nature vs. Nurture." *The Harvard Medical School Mental Health Letter* 2 (October 1985): 5–6.

Money, John. *Gay, Straight and In-Between: The Sexology of Erotic Orientation.* New York: Oxford, 1988.

John Money is the dean of sexologists, and this is the latest in a long series of articles and books. His detailed (and sometimes daunting) research provides an in-depth theory of the development of sexual identity and erotic attraction that he says includes both prenatal and ormonal influences and the effect of certain "critical periods" in early childhood. Most interesting is his theory of "lovemaps," or the "personalized developmental representation or template in the brain that depicts the idealized lover and the idealized program of sexuoerotic activity with that lover as projected in imagery and ideation, or actually engaged in with that lover." In short, lovemaps account for the fact that not all of us are sexually aroused by the same thing: some find men attractive, some women; some are aroused by certain physical builds, or by leather, or by bondage or violence. Money's may not be the definitive theory on the development of sexual identity, but it surely is a solid and provocative beginning.

Morris, D. *Manwatching.* New York: Harry N. Abrams, 1977.

National Conference of Catholic Bishops (NCCB). *To Live in Christ: A Pastoral Reflection on the Moral Life,* U.S. Catholic Conference Publications Office, Washington, D.C. 1976, p. 19.

————. "On Behalf of Voiceless Victims of Injustice: Human Rights and Reconciliation." In *Origins,* November 7, 1974, pp. 318–319.

Nelson, J. *Embodiment: An Approach to Sexuality and Christian Theology.* Minneapolis: Augsburg Publishing House, 1978.

See especially chapter 8, "Gayness and Homosexuality." This is a thoughtful and sympathetic treatment of the issue from a seminary ethics professor in the liberal Protestant tradition. He writes: "I came to believe that acceptance of homosexuality and of its responsible genital expression adequately represented the direction of both the Gospel and contemporary research. While full acceptance means a rather sharp turning from the majority opinion in the Christian moral tradition about homosexuality, I am convinced that it does not mean an ethical change from the central thrust of the Gospel. Rather, it means its fuller implementation"(199).

————. *The Intimate Connection: Male Sexuality, Masculine Spirituality.* Philadelphia: The Westminster Press, 1988.

Nelson's latest book helps men to see that they not only possess a "hard, aggressive" side analogous to phallus but also a "soft, receptive" side analogous to penis. An excellent, innovative approach to spirituality. Good reading for both straight and gay men.

Nugent, R. "Homosexual Catholics: Very Near to God." *Priest* 37 (December 1981): 31–36.

By a co-founder of New Ways Ministries, who is probably the most consistently articulate spokesman for a positive theology of homosexuality.

————. "Homosexuality and the Hurting Family." *America* 144 (February 18, 1981): 154–157.

————. "Courage Curbs Gays." *National Catholic Reporter* 21 (January 18, 1985): 10.

Nugent presents an alternative view to that proposed by John Harvey and offers a critique of the approach Harvey uses with his Courage groups.

————, ed. *A Challenge to Love.* New York: Crossroad, 1983.

Nugent, R., and J. Grammick, S.S.I.D., eds. *A Time To Speak.* Mt. Ranier, MD: New Ways Ministry, 1984.

A chronological collection of contemporary statements on homosexuality, gay ministry, and social justice by U.S. Catholic sources from December 1973 to August 1984. The sources are bishops and archbishops, Catholic newspapers, diocesan commissions, and religious order provincial councils.

Ohanneson, J. *And They Felt No Shame: Christians Reclaiming Their Sexuality.*Winston Press, MN: 1983, pp. 64–65.

Oraison, M. *The Homosexual Question.* Translated by Jane Zeni Flinn. New York: Harper & Row, 1977.

Peck, M. Scott, M.D. *People of the Lie.* New York: Simon & Schuster, 1983).

Pennington, B., O.C.S.O. "Vocation Discernment and the Homosexual." In *A Challenge to Love.* New York: Crossroad, 1984, pp. 235–244.

In this sensitive discussion of how vocation directors should approach gay candidates, Pennington concludes: "Provided, of course, that the particular individual is psychologically healthy and truly opting for celibacy for the Kingdom, I think a gay man who knows and accepts himself can become an excellent religious or priest" (244).

Ratzinger, J. "Letter to the Bishops of the Catholic Church on the Pastoral Care of Homosexual Persons." *Origins*, November 13, 1986.

The most recent official statement to come out of the Vatican on the issue of homosexuality. This document was viewed by some as being directed primarily at Catholic bishops in the United States who, in the view of Vatican officials, may have become excessively tolerant of homosexuality and the "mainstreaming" of gay Catholics.

Redding, M. "Catholic and Lesbian." *Tablet* 237 (January 15, 1983): 30–31.

Presents a perspective similar to that proposed by Brian McNaught, but from a feminine point of view.

Ross, M. "Actual and Anticipated Societal Reaction to Homosexuality and Adjustment in Two Societies." *Journal of Sex Research* 21 (February 1985): 40–55.

Ross examines postulates set forth by Weinberg and Williams (1975) and concludes that homosexual men who have not experienced any specific acts of hostility toward themselves because of their sexuality are more likely to be psychologically troubled than gay men who have had to deal with overt and sometimes violent acts of discrimination.

Rueda, E. *The Homosexual Network: Private Lives and Public Policy.* Old Greenwich, CT: Devin Adair, 1982.

Reuda's work is, without question, meant to alarm conservative-minded individuals about the extent to which homosexuals have gained footholds in every major social institution. His early and consistent reference to the growing influence of the gay community as an "infiltration" betrays his intentions to even the most casual reader. Nonetheless, his meticulous research has produced a volume that is a valuable source book of information for any interested reader.

Sacred Congregation for the Doctrine of the Faith. "Declaration on Sexual Ethics," *Catholic Mind* (April 1976): 52–64.

Salm, L., F.S.C. "The Vow of Chastity and Moral Theology Today." In *Sexuality: A Seminar on Sexuality and Brotherhood.* Edited by Martin Helldorfer. Lockport, IL: Christian Brothers Conference, 1977.

This article appears in a series of articles on sexuality sponsored by the Christian brothers that includes articles by such others as Gabriel Moran and James Zullo. Salm's article makes a nuanced proposal to understand "genital sexual activity as morally justified—and therefore compatible with chastity—so long as it is exercised with responsibility and according to the circumstances." Despite its obvious dissonance with tradition, Salm hopes that it might keep some from "loosing the demonic" in sex that is heavily restrained by external norms, and help them "humanize it [i.e., sex] and tap its full potential for personal and interpersonal growth" (22–23).

Simmel, G., "Conflict." In *Conflict and the Web of Group Affiliations*. New York: Free Press, 1955.

————. "The Stranger." In *On Individuality and Social Forms*. Edited by Donald N. Levine. Chicago: Univ. of Chicago Press, 1971.

Stoller, R., M.D., and G. Herdt, Ph.D. "Theories of Origins of Male Homosexuality: A Cross-Cultural Look." *Arch. Gen. Psychiatry* 42 (April 1985) : 399–404.

Timmermann, J. *The Mardi Gras Syndrome: Rethinking Christian Sexuality*. New York: Crossroad, 1984.

The author identifies a number of conflicting attitudes that have produced a dis-ease or alienation regarding sexuality. As a theologian she shows how the traditional "natural law" approach to morality continues to be characterized by an artificial restraint coupled with periodic overindulgence. Though she does not address the homosexual dimension of human sexuality, she does suggest that a wholesome and responsible integration of sexuality with the rest of life will come through its inner meaning: communication.

Tripp, C. *The Homosexual Matrix*. New York: McGraw-Hill, 1975.

The author's wide-ranging approach to the topic has made this book an invaluable resource for over a decade. His detailed "behind-the-scenes" journalism combines with scholarly research to provide a volume suitable for researchers and casual readers alike.

Wagner, R., O.M.I. *Gay Catholic Priests: A Study of Cognitive and Affective Dissonance*. Ph.D dissertation; Institute for Advanced Study of Human Sexuality. San Francisco, CA: Specific Press, 1981.

Weinberg, M., and C. Williams. *Male Homosexuals: Their Problems and Adaptations*. New York: Oxford Univ. Press, 1974.

This volume reports the analysis of an international study conducted in the early 1970s to examine the impact of social intolerance on the adaptation of behaviors of homosexual men, the first major study of gay men that did not deal with psychiatric patients. The authors provided convincing evidence to authorities in the field of a growing and broad-based homosexual subculture.

Whitehead, James, and Evelyn Whitehead. "The Shape of Compassion: Reflections on Catholics and Homosexuality." *Spirituality Today* 39(1987): 126–136.

A critical evaluation of the 1986 Vatican letter on the care of homosexual persons in which the authors try to provide a corrective to the letter's "coldly rational" tone and overly "biological and naturalistic" view of the person. In this article, the Whiteheads try to build a spirituality of compassion by reminding us that "we are the body of Christ and part of our body is gay and lesbian." For homosexuals and heterosexuals alike, even sexual arousals "can be occasions of grace."

Zullo, J., and J. Whitehead. "The Christian Body and Homosexual Maturing." In *A Challenge to Love*. Edited by Robert Nugent. New York: Crossroad, 1983.

Applies developmental patterns in human life (especially those relating to mid-life) to gay people. An excellent discussion of how we consolidate our sexual and affective identities as we move toward maturity: "During the many seasons of our twenties through our fifties, our instincts of love and anger are seasoned by Christian values and ideals. Our instincts, once so confusing, unruly and unseasoned (think of adolescence!) become more reliable and trustworthy . . . "

Index